Angela Badger was born in the New Forest, Hampshire, England, and in 1970 she emigrated with her family to Australia.

Her work has appeared in *The Sydney Morning Herald* and *The Canberra Times*. One of her early short stories was published by the South Pacific Association for Commonwealth Literature and Language Studies.

Her junior fiction novel, *The River's Revenge*, has been read on Radio National and is in many school libraries.

Now resident in Sydney, she has a keen interest in early Australian history and hopes to pursue this in future work.

*To Kay, Mary and Irene,
with love and gratitude for
their unfailing encouragement.*

The Boy from Buninyong

The Life of an Australian Showman

Angela Badger

VICTORIA PRESS

A Victoria Press Publication

Victoria Press aims to make Victoria, its people, places
and activities a more visible part of our lives, and to
engender pride in the State.

Published by The Law Printer
Melbourne, Victoria, Australia

Address all enquiries to:
The Government Printer for the State of Victoria
PO Box 292, South Melbourne 3205

First published 1993

ISBN 0 7241 8458 9

Mail and bulk order sales:
The Law Printer
28 Queensbridge Street, South Melbourne 3205
Telephone enquiries (03) 242 4600

Written by Angela Badger
Designed by Evie Sampson, Victoria Press
Printed by The Law Printer

Contents

Introduction

Owen Rutherford Lloyd was born in 1907, and I met him when he was sixty-three. He ran a junk shop in the Botany Road and at nights went busking up at the El Alamein Fountain in King's Cross.

Like many of the passers-by, I always paused to look in his window; there were piles of china, old sporting trophies, pots and pans, even a stuffed baby crocodile. The variety was endless.

One day he put his head round the door and called me in. Owen was immaculately dressed, with a shock of white hair. Huge rings flashed on his fingers and his eyes sparkled with the joy of life.

'Want a job?' he asked. I didn't really but I could not resist him or his shop. So I became the junkman's assistant and began to learn about a life which has few parallels.

Owen came from a conventional, middle-class family in Ballarat. During the Depression he lost his apprenticeship and, constructing a fiddle, went busking in Geelong and later Melbourne.

He slipped into the life of a travelling showman. Learning animal training, hypnotism, mind reading, fire eating, sword swallowing, he eventually travelled the show circuits of Australia and New Zealand and even took a circus around east and South Africa.

Owen was not a boaster and I only learnt of his past life from the numerous old show folk who called in to pass the time of day – gypsy fiddlers, African midgets, Maori wrestlers and sideshow operators.

One Sunday I had a phone call from him. His voice was hoarse, his speech slurred. He was feeling groggy he said, would I come over? He thought his end was near, he'd had a 'turn'. As we waited for the doctor he began to reminisce. I listened entranced.

'Wait on,' I said, 'let me get a biro and some paper.'

'Get away,' he said, 'no one's interested in my sort of life.'

There will never be another life like Owen's. As I sat in that chilly room and scribbled furiously I met characters who have long disappeared from this earth but who will remain forever part of Australia's past.

After the doctor had gone I made him a cup of tea. 'You can't die yet,' I told him. 'You haven't told me what happened to Mystic Mora, or how The Handless Wonder lost his hands, or what happened when the camel bit the baby's head off.'

So I embarked on this miraculous journey and Owen kept on living for the sheer pleasure of telling his story.

Chapter 1

Ballarat

I was born in 1907 at Buninyong, a small town in central Victoria. Later, when our family became more prosperous, we moved to nearby Ballarat.

My earliest memory is spending Saturday afternoons hiding in the scrub at the edge of The Miners' Racecourse watching as dozens of pigeons were released from their boxes.

They'd stretch their necks and soar upwards, savouring their freedom. Then the crackle of gunfire split the air and they'd flutter helplessly back to earth. I waited each week hoping to rescue a bird, take it home and nurse it back to life. Occasionally I managed to find one still alive; I'd rush back home with it, spend hours trying to revive the poor creature with warm milk from an eye dropper. But they always died, not a single bird survived.

Each Saturday I heard the men coughing and wheezing as the keen air from Mount Buninyong caught at their throats. The wheezing turned to retching and the retching clawed at them till they choked and spat upon the ground. The older ones were nigh finished, half-dead men at forty, their lungs pierced through and through with fine slivers of silica from a lifetime spent underground.

For this single hour they were men again. For a short while power was theirs, they were the victors, not the vanquished. Jubilantly they shot the terrified birds out of the air and rejoiced against the backdrop of mullock heaps. I would never be a miner.

My best fortune was in my family. Give a child a good family and they won't go far wrong unless there's real evil in that child. My old Dad was a wonderful man, who lived to eighty-four and died within a fortnight of Mother. They were a first-rate pair. I reckon they were parents any family would be proud to have.

Of course they came from good stock. Like a horse, it's the

breeding that counts. Breeding is there right from the start. You can see some people with their shifty low-class ways and you know they only came from rubbish in the first place. They'll never amount to anything in life.

We were 'Good as gold,' my old granny used to say. She reckoned we were a family she could be proud of.

Gold. That's what made us all and that's what made our part of Victoria, too. Bendigo, Buninyong, Castlemaine, Daylesford ... and Ballarat of course.

Ballarat is where it started. Before the first gold was discovered the land had been used for grazing. Then one day some chap was out looking for a lost cow and he came across a piece of quartz shining with gold embedded in it. That started the rush.

A madness seized people. They upped and left their jobs and their families, they flocked to Ballarat. Inside a few weeks from the day of that first find, nearly three thousand men were reckoned to be on the diggings. It cost them thirty shillings a month for their claim, only eight foot square, and they turned the country upside down. Muck and washdirt filthied everything, trees were chopped down for tent poles and fuel, grass disappeared underfoot in a sea of mud. The pastures vanished and mud seeped everywhere. A city of tents spread over the landscape.

People talk about the mess everyone's making of the world these days with all the pollution ... it's always been the same. When there's a bit of money to be made, that's the end of folks' finer feelings. If someone discovered a reef under the Botanical Gardens in Sydney, they'd find an excuse for ripping up the park and Government House too into the bargain.

It didn't take them long to find all the gold which lay around near the surface. By the time they'd picked up the last of it, news had reached the rest of the world that there were fortunes to be made in Australia. That's when people began to think seriously about this country; men who really knew about mining put their minds to the matter. Scots, Welshmen, Cornishmen; tin miners and coal miners who understood what the job was about, men who knew how to sink a shaft and work underground. That was when my crowd came over.

Great Grandfather on father's side, and Lloyd George's

mother, were brother and sister. That's the Welsh side of my family. Great Grandfather married a descendant of Flora Macdonald, the very same who hid Bonnie Prince Charlie and changed the course of history. That's our Scottish side. I never tired of hearing tales of this amazing great grandmother.

Her name was Katherine Macdonald. She'd set off, all on her own, to see what life could hold for her at the other end of the world. She met a Jesuit priest on the ship, named John Moore, fell in love with him and that was the end of his religious duties.

Word had been passed down in our family that she'd married him within a few months, 'fair dizzy with love'. But he was an idle devil, not much taken with the pick or shovel so she had to turn her hand to nursing and midwifery to keep the family going.

Great Grandmother's reward came when Grandad struck it rich in The White Horse Range. He found a reef which was very nearly pure gold, called it The Jeweller's Shop. He set the old folks up in a nice little store in Buninyong so they could end their days in prosperity.

'Your Grandad never took anyone to The Jeweller's Shop. He shared his secret with no one. And there was many another just like him. The men kept tight-lipped about their finds.' Granny never tired talking about their mine. 'Near solid gold, he said it was. Reckoned you could be fair dazzled with the lumps of gold shining in the lamplight. Twenty-four foot square, he said it was.'

The riches of the Jeweller's Shop still lie hidden in the White Horse Range. Grandad was knocked down in the main street of Ballarat by a drunken brewer as he whipped his horses and careered along regardless. The secret died with Grandad.

'No use crying over spilt milk. We searched and we searched but we never came across the place again. So we just managed, like folk do.' Granny often related the tale as we sat round the table on Sunday.

Sunday was a day set apart for ritual. If Saturday had to be spent shivering by the Racecourse looking on hopelessly as humans vented their frustration, then Sunday was the day for putting it all to rights.

There'd be church in the mornings followed by Sunday dinner with roast beef and Yorkshire pudding. Then the house was kept very quiet while Dad had his Sunday nap and my four sisters and I crept out to Sunday School.

Granny always came to tea on Sunday. We'd start the meal with cold meat remaining from the joint, hard boiled eggs and salad. There'd be bread and butter and jam and honey. Mother always baked one of her double-decker sponges; oozing with cream, it towered on its glass stand over the lamingtons, fairy cakes, coconut kisses and rockbuns. Then we'd finish the whole wonderful feast with jelly and custard. Sunday tea put the world to rights again.

Granny was very proud of our Dad. 'Your Dad's got a head on his shoulders,' she never tired of telling us. 'He's never going to die from concrete lungs.'

Concrete lungs was the verdict passed on many a poor dead miner. You could hear men choking their way home at the end of their shift, clinging to the wooden railings of the gardens as they passed, twisted up with agony as they gasped for breath. Once I heard a neighbour whispering to mother, 'When they opened him up his lungs were solid with dust!' I certainly would never be a miner.

Dad had the skill, and the foresight, to improve his lot. After many years underground he was, at forty, a mine manager. His position combined with skilful purchasing of shares in other mines had given him a respected place in the community. But while Granny praised him, Dad always looked to the future and made up his own mind.

'Gold is what made us ... there'll always be gold in Ballarat,' Granny never failed to reminisce.

'Maybe,' Dad would reply, 'but do you know how deep they are working? Why, at South Star they're down 3,000 feet. The men can only stand four hours at a time. The heat's beyond bearing and the pumps are working twenty-four hours a day to keep the water out.'

'A miner's life's always been hard,' Granny would counter.

'Hard! Granted it's always been hard, but mark my words, gold'll get so expensive to get out of the ground they'll have to leave it there.'

'Get away with you,' Granny glanced across at Mother. 'There'll always be gold in Ballarat.'

Dad was right. Gold rose to four pounds an ounce on the

world market, but the cost of getting it out of the ground was eight pounds.

Gold is still there, but in the end it was neither the heat nor the water that finished the mining, it was the cruel waste of men in the First World War. The young men went but so few came back. The older ones were crippled with silicosis and couldn't feed the batteries fast enough to keep goldmining profitable. That was when the cost rose and Ballarat was finished for goldmining.

Chapter 2

Survival and the Noble Art of Self Defence

We shifted to Melbourne after Dad gave up mining; he thought there'd be more future for the family as well as himself. Ballarat had seen the last of prosperity for the time being. Much of Australia was booming and seemed set for the good times, but with the closures of many of the mines in Ballarat, Dad was certain there was no future there.

'You'll need a trade,' he was always telling me. 'If a man's got a trade he'll never want for anything. You've a head on your shoulders and nimble fingers too – engineering is the life for you.'

So engineering it had to be. In those days none of us had that much say regarding what we turned our hands to, you trusted your parents. I'd still trust the old man; he was a fine father, but none of us knew the world was a changing place.

Just as he said, I was going to be an engineer, and I was apprenticed to Mackay's, the big agricultural firm. At first things didn't go badly. Dad was right. I had a head on my shoulders and a way with mechanical things which is still with me to this day. But I never did take kindly to discipline, other than the old man's kind. To be shouted at, to be pushed out of the way and cursed by larrikins who just happened to have half a head in height over me, or were older, or were stronger, was a difficult thing to put up with. I'd emerged into the world of the working man and I didn't much like what I saw.

'Fetch m'spanner,' one of the older lads shouted at me one day. As usual I went off and brought it for him but in the moment of handing it over another whipped it out of my hand and tossed it back to his mate. They tossed that spanner to and fro over my head, all being taller chaps than me, and then by bad luck it fell right on my nose and started it bleeding.

Whether it was the blood or just frustration I'll never know, but I went mad. I laid into those blokes like a fiend, but I had no chance. They kicked and pushed me from one to the other till I hit my head on the bench.

'Here, what's going on!' said the foreman as he came over.

'Young Lloyd's getting cheeky again,' someone said. So on top of it all I had a fair dressing down and had to stand and take it all with the blood dripping down my chin.

There can be a bit too much of that kind of thing, and after a couple of months of being bullied and expected to do all the fetching and carrying like some tame monkey, I decided I'd better do something positive about myself.

'Turn the other cheek,' the scriptures say. That's all very well, but there comes a time when you've got to stand up for yourself, so I took myself off to the YMCA and joined the boxing and wrestling classes.

The YM had a first class gym and I went there each evening after work. Small I might be, but I've got real broad shoulders, proper Welsh stock my old Granny used to say ... a real pit pony, she always called me. My biceps became hard as iron in no time at all; my body seemed to have been waiting for this kind of discipline. Being very quick on the feet and being able to weave and dance like a professional by the time I'd added some science to my punches I felt I could do real damage. But I kept quiet, I didn't let on what I was up to, and waited for my chance.

'Seen yer box?' one of the other apprentices asked me one day, and as he spoke another emptied my lunch box on the ground.

'Wasting his mum's good tucker again,' another one jeered.

But I'll say this, it was the last word he spoke that afternoon. I caught him straight under the jaw and he fell flat on top of the cheese sandwiches they'd scattered around.

'Anyone want any more?' I asked them, 'because they can have it, right here and now.' But they said no more to me, and kept clear of me after that.

*   *   *

At eighteen I had my first real fight, against the undefeated light and welterweight champion of Scotland. Some blokes had found him in a showground booth giving displays and they brought him along. They reckoned they'd give me a quid if I beat him.

I reckon he wasn't too young, and probably if the truth were known the only reason he was unbeaten in Scotland was because he'd never been back. But he understood the art all right. He'd been a good man and could still have laid out most men, but I was on my mettle. I wanted that quid and I was going to have it.

My speciality was the Bob Fitzsimmons Shift ... you lead with your right arm, then your right foot comes up at the same time and you shift your weight, same of course with the left. This puts the whole mass of the body behind the blow and I needed that, being a bit light.

Even so I knew I'd not beat him with my fists; this was a case when you needed brains. So I played a bit stupid first of all. I led him along so he reckoned I was just another kid who thought he knew it all, and I acted very cocky.

I could see this old bloke licking his lips at the thought of the mess he was going to make of my nose. I backed and weaved and feinted until he must have been getting under the weather with exhaustion. Then I shifted myself and let him have it.

A couple of straight lefts, a cross counter and then I finished up with my Bob Fitzsimmons. He was staggering by then, and only the first bell saved him. Next round I didn't even give him a chance to get into me. I just repeated the routine and there he was flat on his back with the crowd roaring. And I can tell you that was the greatest amount of money I'd ever held in my hand, that quid, I reckoned I'd earned it all right.

After that nothing could stop me, I was undefeated. In every bout I wiped the floor with my opponent. In fact I was a fair way into thinking I'd take up the sport and go professional.

Fate has a funny way of pointing her finger though, and if you've got your head stuck on properly you take note. I had a warning one day which no one in their senses would ignore.

A couple of blokes came looking for me, very excited, said there was a chap who wanted to fight me. He'd heard I was undefeated and he reckoned on doing the job. I suppose I was too puffed up at the time, I reckoned no one on this earth could beat me. At eighteen you feel immortal. My body was my God and would deny me no victory.

This bloke they'd found was very quiet, didn't say much at all, and if I'd had my proper senses about me I'd have looked at him a bit closer and thought a little more. He was pale, and not what you'd call in very good shape. I reckoned on him being a real pushover. We met on a mate's property outside of town. Three pounds for the winner and everyone around was placing their bets when I got there. As soon as I saw the glitter in that chap's eyes I knew I'd stepped into something I'd have been best keeping well out of.

Charlie, as they called him, came at me in a way no boxer would. His head down and arms flailing, he hooked me round the ankle and felled me, then he was on me like lightning. Out of the corner of my eye I saw his hand coming down to chop me on the back of the neck like a rabbit. The finish of me was in that bloke's eyes and good sense told me to cut the corners and cut them fast if I ever wanted to see the end of my road.

Letting fly with everything to get away from him I stopped him chopping my neck, but as I struggled with him I sensed he was barely human. His grip was like iron and when I grabbed at him it was more like fighting with a steel cable than a man, a cable which tore at my legs and snapped round my neck. He was all arms, legs, fists and butting head, and he followed no rules. I never knew what to expect next. Again I decided the best thing was to play cautious, weary him and exhaust him and then come in when his strength was wasted. So I went at him in my usual way.

As he followed me around I always kept just far enough away to take the edge off his blows. But this was no ordinary bout, I soon cottoned on to that. The blokes around were staring fascinated, they never once stood up to referee or help me, there were no rounds called. We were against each other till the best man won. But I knew it was not the best man who would win, brute force could triumph if I wasn't careful. Inside I was in a cold fury at the way I'd been tricked. Got out to this lonely place and faced with this bruiser who only wanted to flatten me. I'd been left to battle on my own. I wasn't going to give them the satisfaction of seeing him fell me.

After I'd spun him out for what seemed a lifetime and he was beginning to look befuddled I decided I'd best finish him off. There was murder in his eyes. Out of the corner of his mouth he kept dripping spittle. I balanced myself really carefully and let him have the good old routine. A couple of Bob Fitzsimmons coming close on each other and then my usual follow up. He went down like a tree.

'Go on! Into him! Into him! Go on!' They all shouted at me.

He lay there moaning as I walked away. I didn't say a word to those dingoes. If I had been on the ground instead they'd have had him jumping on me ... I knew that for sure.

I tried to forget the whole thing, but at the back of my mind was an uneasy feeling. Nothing had been clean about that fight. A nasty sneaking suspicion grew that I'd not heard the last of it. A couple of days later my father was waiting when I got home.

'You and I have a visit to make,' was all he said, but he looked very grave.

I'll never forget the place where we went. If God ever meant there to be a hell he chose that place. If there is any music in hell then it is the cries of the poor demented.

That man had not long been out of the asylum. Those blokes had thought it might be a bit of fun setting me up against a madman just to see how I'd make out. They'd amused themselves betting on the outcome ... me a young lad and him not long ago a raving lunatic.

'You'd better see what you've done,' Dad told me.

The chap was lying on a bed, no sheets, no blankets, he was strapped around with coarse fabric which held him tight and was fastened at the back.

'In a straitjacket, poor devil. And do you know he was only let out of this place last Monday? Cured, they said he was, capable of living a normal life again. They say he's taken such a beating from you that this will be his last home.'

I couldn't look that creature in the eyes. I couldn't explain to him or Dad or anyone that I'd not known what I was doing ... never would I have pasted a poor sick human being like that.

I've never been so ashamed of myself in my life. On the other hand if I hadn't stood up for myself I'd have been dead. He'd have killed me and those chaps would have had their sport watching it.

That was the end of boxing for me. Never again did I go into the ring. True, I kept the facility ... defending my rights and looking after my own. Never again did I fight for money or reputation.

*   *   *

Life went bad on me. Tradesmen were being laid off and finally Mackay's terminated my apprenticeship. We were not yet in the Depression, but even so, work was hard to find.

Being out of work at my age was a slap in the face. To look at the older men and their bent bodies, and then to look at my own strong arms and legs and think I was in the same boat as them was degrading. I began to lose confidence in myself. I'd always accepted Dad's plans without question – he knew the best. I'd have been a first class engineer, I knew that, he knew it too, but the world did not care one jot. A door had shut on me.

More fortunate than some, I finally found work on the colliers going out of Melbourne. It was not much of a job, no future in it, but there's nothing like a bit of cash to keep the spirits up.

They were a mixed crowd aboard the *SS Werribee*, but by now I could take the rough with the smooth to my complete satisfaction. I was a bit more cautious by then, I kept myself to myself until I came across an English deckhand who used to play a one-string fiddle. I'd always been very fond of music; my sister Olwen was a wonderful pianist and Grandfather had conducted all the local orchestras around Ballarat in his young days, but I'd never had an opportunity to learn much about the subject.

This bloke would bring his fiddle out in the evening and sit on the deck, playing just for the sheer pleasure, and everyone would gather round for a real singsong. Those were good times, not much inducement to squander your money. Most of the time you couldn't anyhow, because you were at sea.

There was good fellowship among the crew and I was fascinated by this man with his fiddle. I studied the instrument very carefully ... it wasn't an ordinary fiddle by any means. The chap was really handy, he'd constructed it himself from a lovely deep brown wood, and at the end was a large horn. When he played the tone that came from it was wonderfully deep and melodious.

I'd make myself one. If he could do it I was sure I could too.

11

My fingers were itching to get on with some work more skilled than scrubbing decks. And it was just as well I had begun to think along those lines because not long afterwards I was paid off from the *SS Werribee*.

This time the whole family's situation was becoming serious. Dad was on the dole, and Mother no longer sang as she worked in the kitchen. She had no time for me, spending all my days down the end of the garden in the shed.

Each morning I hurried down there and worked on that fiddle. From the remains of an old china cabinet I constructed what in my eyes was a masterpiece, an excuse too, an excuse to keep me from joining the dole queue.

'You've no feelings, Owen ... do you think it's any better for your poor father? You're in a dream world down there ... fooling around making that wretched fiddle of yours. You'd best face the facts because I'm telling you this ... when you can't pay your way ... out you go! We've enough mouths to feed as it is, without a young chap like you standing on your dignity.'

I didn't answer. What could I say? That I'd spent days fitting the sections of wood a mate had cut on his bandsaw for me, that I'd made fittings at each end from some bits of brass I'd found on Dad's bench and now all I was left with was attaching the old gramophone horn which I'd found down on the dump.

Certainly the construction didn't look very impressive, but I was working on it and I'd made up my mind that the fiddle would be completed soon and that I would play those haunting tunes the English sailor had conjured up for me. And I'd make a living at it too.

That fiddle took me nearly a month in the end. Once finished I sat for hours trying to recapture the tunes which were still spinning round in my head. I should have spent much longer perfecting them, but time was not on my side. I'd reckoned that I needed a couple of good old melodies and so I concentrated upon 'Loch Lomond' and 'Nelly Dean'. They were tunes which I could hum to myself and at the same time pick out the notes.

When I'd got them well into my head I felt fear rising inside me for the first time. Could I do it? Could I turn my back on all I knew and take such a chance? My family had been so respectable, good old mining stock slowly bettering itself, painstakingly climbing up the ladder of convention to a respected place in society. Would I be laughed at, would I be the object of scorn and pity?

The world would shortly be looking at me and I might appear a pathetic sight. But when I stood in that queue for the dole I would be looking at myself and I knew, right to the very core, that I'd really be pathetic then. If the world laughed at me that was a darned sight better – the world did not matter as much as I did.

The more I thought, the stronger the resolve grew inside me, and finally I took my fiddle and got a lift out to Geelong. On no account would I perform in Melbourne or anywhere near the family. I'd go where I knew no one.

I chose a nice little park, fairly near the centre of town, with no police around because I wasn't too sure how I stood with them. I sat down and unwrapped the fiddle, never feeling so exposed in all my life, sitting there all alone with the whole world around me. I felt everyone was looking at me and I did not even know how to play properly. I was scared stiff, I kept my eyes on the instrument because the panic that was rising inside had blurred the streets, the park and the buildings all around.

Still keeping my head down I started off with 'Loch Lomond'. The sounds which had filled our shed just dissolved into the space of that park. But I carried on, I'd made up my mind that I'd sit there all morning and just see what turned up. If I failed then the time had come to join Dad in the queue.

'Look at that beggar over there!' I heard a child call, and looked over my shoulder to see where he was pointing. He was pointing at me. The blood rose in my face so I did not look up again and after a while I heard the clatter of money falling upon the pavement.

The sound of that money was the most wonderful thing I'd heard for a long while. When you've not held a paypacket in your hands for longer than you'd like to remember the clink of coins is as good as the sweetest music.

I made six shillings that first day. The hardest six shillings I've ever earned, because I had to swallow my pride and that is the most difficult thing for a young man.

But there was another side. During the dejection of the last weeks, I had enjoyed making that fiddle, my mind had been occupied and my hands put to some use, and even if I could only play those two tunes I savoured every note and each time played them a little more surely. Getting the tune a mite more perfect each time became a challenge, each time a little better ... just a little better.

I'll never forget the look on Mother's face when I handed her the six shillings. She didn't say a word. She was upset for me, for herself, for the family; she knew what it had cost me to earn that money. I'd had to master my pride. But what could a fellow do? Stand around, hold his hand out for the dole with no hope for the future, not even a glimmer of times getting better. No, that wouldn't be my way. Never give up! Never let the world ride you, I say. Just keep on trying, and as one door closes so another will open. Something always turns up.

Getting to Geelong each day was a chancy business, and even though time passed rapidly and I began to feel quite at home on the streets, I still didn't want the family to see me earning my money. So I decided to look for lodgings. I could afford them well enough now.

I paid no more than a shilling a night. No good being too fussy, but I wasn't going to stop in one of those bloodhouses where the bugs turned you into mincemeat inside the first night. My first lodgings were rough and ready, nothing like home, but cheerful enough.

'You'll be having company,' the landlady said when she opened the bedroom door. 'There's Patrick over there, next to the washstand.'

Afterwards I realised I'd been lucky only to have two beds in the tiny room. The last one in had to shift for himself if we wanted the door closed. I kept my fiddle on top of the lowboy in case Patrick stumbled on it during the night.

This Patrick was a Paddy. A tinker by trade, he went round the streets mending pots and pans. Skinny, and none too clean in his ways, he had the most shocking set of teeth I'd ever laid eyes on, and on account of his bad breath he was never without a peppermint in his mouth. Reckoned it cleared away the stink of his gums and teeth.

Patrick was full of advice, seeing that I was obviously a newcomer to lodging houses of any sort, and he was an expert in the art of managing landladies and coaxing the best out of them. I was very innocent then, I can see it now, but quick to learn all the same.

I hadn't been there long when another lodger arrived, a fortune teller by the name of Madame de Rossi. She was a very tall, striking woman who made a good living at the cards. Always tidy, well shod and not a strand of hair out of place except for kiss curls over her ears. She had more style than any woman I'd come close to before.

Madame de Rossi had real talent. Many a time we'd sit around in the kitchen and the landlady would call her neighbours in, they'd bring their friends and relatives too. What Madame could tell those people about their private lives and characters was quite amazing. The kitchen fast became a regular meeting place, and some nights I'd fetch down my fiddle and we'd end up with a proper singsong.

'Can't yer hold yer noise,' that Paddy would yell after we'd been going for a bit. He was a great one for getting his head down early.

'That Patrick's a common sort of man,' Madame de Rossi said to me. 'Can't think why you share a room with him.'

'Not much chance of anyone else to share with,' I replied giving her a look. But she wasn't having any, being a respectable woman going on for thirty and not inclined to getting a bad name for herself.

I've always been a fairly respectful type. If they don't want you then you abide by their wishes, that's my motto. In point of fact I've never spent a lot of time with women. They spell trouble for men like me. I'm a travelling man.

My being a bit shy and timid seemed to goad her on. She began to dress a trifle flashily, wore some little charm bracelets that tinkled and rattled in the most delicate way when she dealt the cards. There was something very enticing about her white hands and those little gold charms. All the time she had her eye on me, I knew that.

We began to get very friendly, Madame de Rossi and me. Sometimes, come the weekend, I'd take her down to the park and we'd have supper at a cafe and it wasn't very long before she was telling me what an extra nice bloke and how clever I was, and what with me and my fiddle and her and the cards, we'd make a good living travelling together. If I played my tunes that would attract the customers and she could tell their fortunes. There was a mint of money to be made on the showgrounds.

I was wondering about all this and whether she might not be a bit too old for me when the Paddy spoke up, very businesslike.

'We'd better see what's in her bank book before you go committing yourself,' he told me. 'There's many a marriage fallen apart because of financial problems. Now, you're a careful lad, always saving and sending home to your mum. It'd be best if she's the same way inclined.'

So we agreed one night I'd take her outside to look at the moon and he'd nip up to her room and see what was in her bank book. He came downstairs with a face as long as a boot.

'She'd be a millstone round your neck Owen,' he told me. 'Not just nothing in it, there's figures in red too and that means only one thing. She's a spender and she'll ruin youse.'

But by now I could only think of her flashing eyes and those lovely white arms. I was beyond caring about ordinary matters like money. About that time I had to go back to see Dad. He wasn't too well, so I left in a hurry and came back just as unexpectedly.

Do you know what I found? Those two canoodling in no uncertain fashion. I was disgusted and told her straight she was not the woman for me. If she wanted that Paddy she could have him.

'I was doing youse a favour,' the Paddy said. 'I just couldn't stick seeing a young lad like you led astray. She's just taking advantage of you, leading you on. It just shows what kind of female she is. If you marry her then you're heading for a packet of trouble.'

Next she came to me. She was all sad and sorrowful, telling me she'd been so lonely without me and she'd been tempted and nothing like that would happen again because I was the most wonderful man she'd ever met and we'd be a happy couple yet. So we went back as we were before, stronger than ever. I even stopped sending Mother any money about that time – I was saving up for a good, solid, gold ring. She was going to have the best ring money could buy, and I kept my cash well hidden inside my belt for safety's sake, not trusting that Paddy in my heart of hearts.

'How about coming to Ringwood along of me?' he asked one day. 'Change would do you good, there's a fair deal of money thereabouts. I always travel in that direction just before Christmas to catch the trade.'

Paddy was a great one for following the trade round the countryside. Reckoned that once you'd worked through one town's pots and pans it was time for the next town's to be going into holes. He often went off for a spell then came back to our lodgings to catch up with the city trade.

I should have thought a bit harder about that Paddy. He was a wild fellow, erratic in his ways, but I put that down to him having lived a wandering life and that making him a bit rougher than most.

'Won't waste our money on lodgings, seeing as the weather's so good,' he said, and suggested we slept out.

'I know a nice little gully just off the road. We can camp down there after we've had our tea and no one will bother us. I've often stopped down there.'

So we had a bite to eat in town and made our way out to the gully. The sky was extra specially bright that night, the stars more like a white mist round the moon than individual stars.

'This is the life,' I told myself, 'sleeping out under the night sky with your mate. A good meal in your belly, your fiddle alongside and a nice wad of money tucked up snug inside your belt.' A rare feeling, that. It seemed I was on my way at last, managing my own life and looking forward to all that happiness with Madame de Rossi.

It must have been getting cloudy; certainly a chill was beginning to settle and seep into my bones. The next thing I remember was lying there looking up at pitch darkness, with no stars anywhere and feeling somehow uneasy.

Something wasn't right and yet for the life of me I couldn't make out what. The money was still inside my belt, my fiddle was by my side. Had some sudden noise woken me up or was it only the coldness of the night air?

The faint scraping of someone slithering over the ground caught my ears and I'd opened my mouth to call for Patrick when hands gripped around my neck like a vice.

Someone had their thumbs dug right into the artery in my neck but as I started to cry out for that tinker to come and help I caught the smell of his accursed peppermint. That rotten Paddy was trying to finish me off.

I'd never let on about the YM and the boxing. I'd never thought to mention it and he'd not have guessed, me being quite a small young chap. There wasn't going to be an opportunity to use real skill, not a chance of the old Bob Fitzsimmons, that was for sure. So I let him get himself nicely onto my throat and he almost relaxed as though he'd found an easy target and was just getting stuck in.

Then I let him have it! A quick half roll loosened the grip. I was on him like a tiger. I caught him round the side of the head with one fist and threw myself right on top of him. I flattened him! I let him have it. No science that night. No need for science really, for that ignorant Paddy was a sitting duck.

I flew at him quickly and brutally and soon he was howling. Then I laid his nose open and he was hanging on to one ear when I kicked him up the backside and went on kicking right down the road and threw his miserable bundle after him.

I had no more sleep that night. I hunched myself under my blanket with my back against a great boulder and watched and waited. He might come back with a knife. He was that sort of dingo. But he didn't, he'd had enough of me. Next morning the reason for camping in that gully was as clear as the daylight. Further up the hillside was the old poppet head of a deserted shaft, thick boronia bush covering the entrance. That's where he reckoned on dumping me that night. With my money under his belt and no evidence of where I'd gone he'd have been back to Madame de Rossi in no time at all telling her I'd shot through.

Did she know though? Was she a cunning woman who'd be getting the best of both worlds? My savings and a steady earning husband. I never knew because I didn't relish going back to the lodgings again. No use getting into situations which you don't fancy or even understand.

Years later I heard he'd married her. Perhaps she had more in that bank book than he let on. They set up a little hardware store and he kept her busy with ten children. All I can say is 'good luck' to the woman, taken in so easily by a wicked, ignorant Paddy. She deserved all she got, but no one was going to lay their hands on my money and I'd learnt a very useful lesson at the outset of life. To be a bit more cautious in dealing with people and think twice, then three times, then think again, before I ever trusted anyone.

Chapter 3

Con Men ... not Forgetting the Ladies,
Sword Swallowing, Fire-Eating and
Positive Thinking

Humans can think, plan, connive and premeditate. You have to be careful when dealing with animals, as I learned later in life in the circuses, but handling humans is far more tricky.

I've met some very bad people in my time; some of them were real savages. You can't learn too quickly to be wary of humans, and that's where a bit of judgement comes in. If you know what's what in life you can sum up a person better and be forewarned.

Should you meet a well-spoken bloke in poor circumstances with a hard luck story, don't just feel sorry for him. At the back of your mind wonder a bit and consider. 'What brought him down?' ... 'Why hasn't he got any friends?' ... and you may save yourself a lot of trouble later.

Look at a man's eyes, look at his hands. Shakespeare said you could tell a man's character by his hands. Look at the way he holds himself. There are a thousand ways of telling what he's made of. Don't let first appearances fool you though. Take note of them and keep on looking.

The biggest eye-opener I ever had was when I met a bloke called Bluey Deane up in Brisbane when I was stopping over at the Salvos. It was years after I'd come across that Paddy.

The Army hostel is a fine place to stay when you're a bit down on your luck and I'd settled myself in there to mark time during a bad patch. Nice people, good tucker, but of course you rubbed shoulders with a very mixed class of people. I was highly gratified to see that the bloke in the next bed looked pretty clean and tidy and beside his pillow he'd laid out the Bible. A decent sort of bloke, I decided.

'You're lucky you've met up with him at the Salvos,' one of the others told me. 'If you'd come across Bluey anywhere else he'd have taken the fluff out of your pockets and the holes out of your socks ... but he never touches no one when they're staying with the Salvos.'

Seems this Bluey was a wonderful pickpocket. He had real class. Travelling as I did over the years I often bumped into him and got to know him pretty well. He told me he'd gone off to New Zealand as a lad to be trained by the famous Scobie Ryan. Scobie Ryan instructed the best con men and pickpockets of all time. People went to him from all over the world.

It seems that when I met Bluey he was very down on his luck. He was back at the bottom of the ladder and getting up the will to work his way back to the top again, grumbling all the time about the poor pickings in Queensland.

'Why don't you go back to New Zealand?' I asked.

'Never leaving Aussie again mate,' he replied, looking a bit fidgetty. He was decidedly jumpy for such a big chap, who should be quite able to look after himself. He was six foot tall with gingery hair, quite a figure of a man.

'What about the States?' I suggested. At that he seemed to shrivel before my eyes. His shoulders drooped and his red hair looked lifeless.

'Not on your life, just come back from there.'

'You must have made some cash to get that far.'

'Fair living.'

'Come off it Bluey ... everyone knows the States is where the money is.'

'You seem interested?' He regarded me closely.

'Often wondered about the place meself.'

'You'd be a bloody fool if you did. Cut out your tripes, they would. There's that many's out of work over there, they'd kick you off the streets, take your fiddle first, of course.'

'Aw ... go on!'

'It's the truth I'm telling you. What rackets aren't run by the Mafia are in the hands of the cops, and half the cops belong to the Mafia anyhow.'

'That's just a line.'

'A line is it?' His eyes glinted.

'Well go on,' I urged him, because even then he hesitated.

'Well, it was like this. I made a fair deal working round the fairs and shows here, not to mention some regular work around the hotels in Sydney. In fact I was beginning to get things too easy. Thought I was wasting my time on the small stuff. Suppose you could say I was getting big ideas. So I decided to try my hand in the States where everyone says the money is.

'I settled in one of their cities, I won't tell you the name of the place,' he looked around nervously, 'and in that particular place I was doing a treat. The cops were in on everything and they had the sweetest system I'd ever come across. If they knew someone was coming to town with a well stacked wallet they'd tip me off ... took about ten percent. All except for one sergeant. He was a regular swine. If he tipped me off he wanted fifty percent and I wasn't having any of that, I told him straight.

'But believe me, you can't get the better of those Yankee cops, they've got the system all sewed up to suit themselves. Our boys are like babes at the breast compared with them. This cop began to get nasty, but I hadn't the sense to think ahead. One day he tips me off a real good one, said he'd do me a favour for once to show there was no ill-will. He told me there's a bloke coming to town, a professional gambler, he'd have a fortune in his vest pocket.'

Bluey shook his head sadly. 'Never again will I trust a cop. I soon caught up with the bloke he'd told me about. Shortish and quite ordinary looking. I followed him all day but didn't chance him because he seemed to be looking around all the time, jumpy like, never settling anywhere. Wore dark glasses, very twitchy, kept his hand in his pocket all the time and always peering over his shoulder.

'Of course these were very good signs, he was obviously carrying a bundle. So I was patient, finally caught up with him at the zoo of all places. He was standing there watching the lions being fed and for a moment not bothering about anything else. So I dipped him quick.'

As Bluey spoke beads of sweat sprang up all over his forehead. 'And do you know who I'd dipped?'

'No,' I said 'how should I know?'

'Babyface Nelson. One of their biggest gangsters.' He was breathing heavily. 'Oh my God, I can tell you I'd have given anything to put that wallet back. He hadn't seen me and it was only when one of me mates told me that some punk had gone over Babyface at the zoo and he and his boys were out looking that I realised what I'd done. I'd fallen right in, that crooked cop had set me up. I wasn't paying him enough and he wanted me off his patch. By the time he'd told Babyface exactly what I looked like and where I hung out and all the rest I'd be at the bottom of the river wearing concrete boots.'

'What did you do?'

'I shot through that night. I skedaddled out of that town so fast I didn't even have time to get me deposit box out of the bank and there was some very nice jewellery in it, not to mention a thousand dollars I'd saved. But I reckoned my life was more to me than any cash, so I left. And do you know what happened?'

'Tell me.'

'Well, I decided only last year that things might have settled down a bit. I still didn't fancy going back there so my sister Amelia went instead. She's always been a good sister to me and we decided no one would connect us, our names being different. She went back to the bank and got the deposit box out and do you know what?'

'No.'

'It was empty. Cleaned right out it was except for a little note. "BE SEEING YOU" it said.

'She came back on the next boat. None of my family's going to go over there again. I don't really feel safe myself, not even here, those gangsters never give up. Just like the cops too, all connected to the Mafia. Gangsters! Crooked cops! America's not a nice place at all.'

So, as I was saying, you can't always judge a man by first appearances. Bluey seemed as nice a gentleman as you could find but he had fingers as light as thistledown.

Then there was the great Scobie Ryan himself. A master of his art. He always insisted on everyone he taught doing things the 'correct way'. He did not hold with slipshod habits, always said that was how you ended up in the cooler. If a job was worth doing it was worth doing properly.

Pickpocketing was his speciality. Always said the best system was to work in threes. Number One attracts the attention of the mark, Number Two dips the pocket and passes the wallet back to Number Three. Number Three runs off with it. All the while Number One is keeping the mark occupied. Asking the way to 'such and such street', or how to get to the railway station.

That routine can be worked till it runs smooth as clockwork. I remember watching three women on that little game all the way along Collins Street one busy Christmas Eve.

'Have you seen my little lad ... I've lost him.' Number One comes sobbing up to the mark, she pointed this way and that in the crowd asking him if he could help her. 'Can you see if he's over there, blue jersey he's wearing, he's carrying a parcel. If you could just look down there ... I'll keep my eyes on the other side of the street.'

Then Number Two dipped the wallet and Number Three showed a clean pair of heels.

'There he is! Over there by that cakeshop. Oh thank you for being so kind and helping me keep an eye open.' And she'd disappear into the crowd. Those women were real professionals.

There are a couple of advantages in working like that. If Number Two is unlucky and is suspected then when they search her the money isn't to be found as its already been slipped to Number Three. If the worst comes to the worst and the bloke gets rough then there are three to take him on.

If there's a dust-up one of the ladies would say the man had made immoral advances and some kind people in the crowd came to her aid ... ten to one the poor old mark is hauled off by the cops and by the time his story's sorted out everyone is well away.

Picking pockets is an art, like the dice or the cards. It never appealed to me but many a good laugh I've had watching that particular game. I've seen some smart thieves and con men in my time.

There was a couple named Slippery Bill and Little Mavis who worked The Diamond Ring Trick all round Victoria and New South Wales, and may still be doing it for all I know. Little Mavis was always dressed a treat and Slippery Bill was a real gentleman. They'd pick a first class hotel in a country town and stop there the night. Never stinted themselves, ordered a slap-up dinner, plenty of wine, coffee and liqueurs too, and Bill would insist on his nightcap of a whisky and soda.

Next morning it would be bacon and eggs for breakfast for

Mavis and a steak for Bill. Then they'd pack their bags and Bill would go to pay the account.

He'd reach for his wallet ... then the fun started.

'My God! I've been robbed!' He'd clap his breast pocket, his coat pocket, his trouser pocket. Red in the face, almost speechless, he'd turn out the bags.

'What's the matter my love?' Mavis would have followed him down by now.

'I've been robbed, all our money's gone!'

'Your wallet's gone?'

'Everything?'

'Even little Peter's ... Peter's photo.' He'd put his arm around her waist and whisper across to the publican, 'Kept a lock of our little son's hair in my wallet ... poor little lad. There, there, my love.' He'd pat her shoulder and then she'd bury her head in her hands.

The landlord would be very uncomfortable; after all his house didn't look a very nice sort of place at all. Little Mavis would struggle to hold back the tears, carrying on all the while about paying the bill before they left. The landlord wouldn't even press too hard, he might suggest they could send the money on to him.

'Oh no, no,' she'd insist. 'Never let it be said we don't settle up. But all I can suggest is this ring I've got.'

She had a real cracker of a diamond ring. She'd flash it under the landlord's nose. 'It's probably quite good, I can't really swear to it though. My auntie left it to me in her will. If you'd care to buy it off me then we can settle the bill and we'd be ever so much happier, wouldn't we my love?'

Bill would nod and act embarrassed.

'If you think it would be acceptable then we'll do that,' she'd continue. 'Of course I've no idea how much it's worth so perhaps someone would care to run along to the jewellers and get it valued.'

So the landlord would take the ring down the street to the local jeweller and watchmaker.

That ring was worth over a hundred pounds. One and a half carats of the first water. Well, human nature being what it is, that chap would probably come back and say it was worth about fifty pounds. Mavis would go all sad and weepy again at the thought of parting with dear old auntie's ring, while Slippery Bill would look like a real high class gentleman who's a bit upset at having to get into such sordid dealings as selling diamond rings to publicans.

'Never mind me,' Mavis would sob. 'Just take our board and lodging out of the money and give us the change. My mind'll never be easy if we leave without settling up. But I wonder if I could ask a favour?'

And the landlord would always agree, they were such nice people.

'Could I just put it on once more ... just for old times sake.' He'd give it back to her and she'd slip it on her finger and sigh a bit while he was taking the fifty pounds out of the till.

Quick as a flash she'd slip a cheap paste copy from her sleeve and palm the real diamond ring away. She would hand over the imitation.

'Here you are. It's a happy ending after all isn't it. So long as you are satisfied. Never mind about what's happened, no one can blame you at all. You can't know everyone you've got under your roof.'

Bill would take the fifty pounds, pay the publican and still have a sizeable wad to put in his pocket.

'Many thanks for your kindness and consideration,' Bill would say and off they'd go.

They got rid of more paste rings than I've had hot dinners. The public are shockingly greedy, can't resist a bargain, and that's when the cons get them.

*   *   *

I've always been very cautious with strangers, and that early experience with the Paddy probably saved me more than I'll ever know.

About that time I decided to start working on the streets of Melbourne. I suppose I'd toughened up inside. I no longer minded who saw me sitting playing in the street. Mother and Dad never commented either. I had slipped into a way of life which suited me, I liked the changing scene, the passing crowds and the noise and bustle.

My repertoire had increased, and now I gave the people their money's worth, all right. I was good enough to tackle the city and try my luck for the first time in Collins Street. You'd be surprised how interested people were in my fiddle playing. I wasn't a handsome bloke but they seemed to take to me and liked to stop for a chat.

That was something useful I learnt early, too. Let people talk about themselves, that's their favourite subject of conversation. Give them their heads, let them tell you about their old mums and dads, their wicked uncles who altered the family will and made off with the cash and their ungrateful children. When they've talked themselves out it's your turn. You've got them in your hand because by now they think, 'He's a good sort, an understanding kind of person.' But it's them that's convinced themselves. By that time they're softened up and half way to believing anything you tell them.

One day a tall bloke came up to where I was sitting, a commanding kind of man with penetrating eyes.

'How are you?' I asked as I usually did when I finished my piece. He was just standing there watching me, not putting anything into my little box.

'Passing fair,' he replied and took out his wallet.

I was watching him like a hawk. Never before had anyone taken out their wallet for me. He pulled out a ten shilling note and I stretched out my hand to take it; I nearly had my fingers round it when it was gone! Instead he was holding a playing card, the Queen of Hearts. I nearly dropped my fiddle with the shock.

He didn't look at me straight, but huffed and puffed a bit as though I'd been rather clumsy and took out another note. The same thing happened again. This time instead of the ten shilling note he handed me the Jack of Hearts.

'Here!' I said, 'why'd you do that?'

'Same reason as you're doing what you've just been doing ... earning a living.'

And that's how I met Dr Richard Rowe. He was the greatest card sharp of all time. I think he was Australian, but I'm not sure. If so Australia should be proud of a man like him.

Dr Richard Rowe was a manipulator who made most people look like a crowd of old folk playing euchre. He was a genius who hasn't been equalled in my lifetime. All his life he was improving his repertoire and to this end he travelled the world ... America, Europe, Africa, everywhere he went he was never out of pocket. He paid his way right round the world several times over and always had enough to buy further knowledge wherever he went.

I learnt a tremendous lot from Dr Rowe. He could saw a lady in half better than any I've met since, and although I learned the art from him I'll honestly say I've never equalled his suave presentation. The Indian Rope Trick, The Cup and Balls, Mind Reading ... he had learnt them all. He told me he always paid a good price for a trick; he made sure he was taught by the masters.

Dr Rowe learnt most of them in India, where the very best illusions come from.

Palming and sleight of hand are an art, but besides that those Indians have a wonderful power over their minds and bodies. They know how to use the will to control the body. Mind you, there were some tricks no Westerner would face, but Dr Rowe reckoned it was worth the money just to see them.

An Indian came up to him one day when he was standing on the banks of the Ganges. The man said he had a very good trick to show him, extra specially good.

'Two annas,' offered the doctor.

'Only for four annas will I do this.'

Dr Rowe agreed and slipped him the money, but being a determined sort of man he palmed back the two annas he did not feel like parting with.

This Indian dived into the river and Dr Rowe stood on the bank and watched him. Right down went the man and the doctor thought he must have drowned he was down so long, so be bent over the bank peered into the water.

The Indian's backside came floating up to the surface and he squirted out a jet of water at the doctor. Just like a fountain, it soaked him to skin.

'My oath I was furious,' Dr Rowe told me. 'I could have strangled the bastard, but in a way I'd deserved it. He must have seen me slipping the two annas. I'd seen a first class trick, not one I'd emulate, but even so it was well worth seeing. So I gave him the two annas and that was the end of it. The man was quite conversational on the subject ... explained he had trained his bowels to take in water and expel it like a pump. Never seen that done before or since.'

Dr Rowe was in partnership with his wife, Mystic Mora. Mystic Mora was a difficult woman, given to moods and fancies, as can only be expected with her being so spiritual. She took a fancy to me. Sometimes I wonder why lady fortune tellers and seers always take to me, because in a way I'm not very happy with them. They are usually difficult women, but perhaps they see a power in me which complements their own.

She wasn't only spiritual, though. She was also very artistic and had a unique act portraying scenes and people in coloured sands. Taking handfuls of different coloured sand out of a number of boxes she'd let it trickle through her fingers into a tray. All the time suitable music would be playing and the picture took shape before the audience's eyes in no time at all. She was a superb show-woman, judged everything to a nicety. If she was making a portrait of The Kaiser then she'd have a military march playing in the background, if she was showing a pretty fountain and sweeping lawns then it would be 'In a Monastery Garden'. She was an artist to her fingertips.

Mystic Mora told her husband that he'd best introduce me to some of their audiences as I would attract business, being young and musical. She could make her pictures to the accompaniment of my fiddle. Far more satisfactory than having Dr Rowe winding up the gramophone behind the screen. And that began a new life for me, not so chancy as sitting on the streets waiting for the wind of generosity to loosen people's purse strings.

'You can't possibly be introduced at the places where we entertain dressed like that,' she told me quite straight. 'We don't patronise the hoi polloi ... our audiences are quite a different class.'

Mystic Mora was an Englishwoman and very upper class for her line of business. She never even tried to understand the life of ordinary people. Nearly everybody belonged to the 'hoi polloi' so they didn't count and the remainder were always perfectly right and beyond reproach.

'I've only got this suit,' I explained, and that was the truth.

'Then we'll advance you some money and you can find something a little more artistic.'

They started me off around some of the local schools. We performed in aid of the funds and then took a small fee for ourselves. Children are a wonderful audience. I'd never played to them on their own before; in fact I'd never faced a hallful of people at all, and I'm glad I began with schools because those laughing faces gave me a lot of confidence.

My first serious engagement with the Rowes was at a garden party in Toorak. Toorak was a favourite area for them, the surroundings made Mora feel quite at home, she said, reminded her of the Old Country and her family's place, somewhere outside London.

Living as I had been up till then either in Ballarat or an ordinary suburb in Melbourne, and then taking myself around lodging houses and country hotels, I'd not realised there was quite another life to be lived.

The house we went to wasn't just a house, it was a small fortress which stretched out through archways and along paths to greenhouses, stables, tennis courts, courtyards and distant summerhouses. You would have got lost just fetching in the mail.

'How do we get paid?' I asked the doctor, for it was unlikely that those gentlemen in their smart suits and ladies in their floating dresses and picture hats would ever drop a few pence in my box.

'Shhh.' Mystic Mora was shocked at my commonness. 'This is for charity.'

I didn't say anything, but I wished I'd known because I'd not have bothered to come. The only charity which really interested me was strictly Owen Rutherford Lloyd. Lucky I didn't let on because the next moment her husband told me that the hostess was going to settle up afterwards. The guests were all contributing to some good cause or other and we'd get our cut out of the proceeds. We had to look as if money was the last thing we were thinking of.

A marquee had been erected on the lawn and inside were trestle tables covered with damask cloths. Champagne glasses clustered at one end and a butler with a shirt so stiff he must have tied his bootlaces before ever getting his clothes on, was meticulously polishing some crystal bowls.

'Come away,' hissed Mora. Peering was vulgar.

But I couldn't take my eyes off that spread. Plates of fish in aspic, pastry cases filled with mushrooms and bits of chicken, caviar dotted all over the place, half a dozen trout decorated with creamy pink and green rosettes, plates of ham and chicken and rare beef; and up on a stand, above the lot, was a great black boar's head, tusks and all, with an apple in his mouth. One of my mates had worked for a pastrycook and I'd heard all about these spreads but I'd never seen one in all my life.

'Rather ostentatious,' said Mora, but ostentatious or not I'd have given a good deal to get myself outside that lot.

We were a great success. Mora was put in a little room they called 'the study' and guests consulted her as they wished concerning their fortunes. Dr Rowe and myself were given a dais against the wall of the house and began our act.

I played my Scottish melodies and then proceeded with an Irish jig. Dr Rowe then came forward and performed his card tricks. He had cards appearing from everywhere and the audience were quite mystified, but there was no magic in it, that's for sure. Just real hard work and practice.

Then out came Mystic Mora. After the coloured sands which gave a very artistic air to the act, she assisted Dr Rowe with his mind reading. I would blindfold him, and with his back turned to her she would then choose someone from the audience and ask her husband to describe them. No one ever guessed how they did it.

They had a code. But because some smart person might break it the code was varied for each person they chose. They had up to ten versions between them and worked them in very strict sequence.

Mora might start off by saying 'Who have I here beside me?' Well, in Code Number One, if she started with the word 'who' that meant a lady. Then she'd say 'Tell me the colour of her dress?' Dr Rowe would say 'blue' because in Code Number One it was a rule that whatever item was mentioned in the second question, it had to be blue. So if the woman had not got a blue dress but instead blue eyes or a blue ring, Mora would say, 'Tell me the colour of the lady's eyes,' or 'what colour is the stone in the ring on her finger?'

Then when the second person came from the audience, Mora might begin with, 'Can you tell me ... ?' In Code Number Two if she began with 'can', that would indicate an elderly gentleman was the subject.

They had tricks galore and kept the session up in the most breathtaking fashion, pretending to guess and get into difficulties. Dr Rowe would clasp his hands to his head and stagger about as though forcing his mind to communicate, and Mystic Mora would breathe hard, nearly collapse, ask for a glass of water, then she'd sigh and groan as though her brain was being pierced with force waves from her husband's consciousness.

Mora was a powerful woman, but not one you could exactly be comfortable with.

*   *   *

When Mother saw my pinstripe suit and two-tone shoes she bit her lip. She was certain I'd got into the wrong sort of company. Try as I might she refused to come and see us perform, even when I told her how we were working round the schools, taking half for ourselves and leaving half for their funds, and how most of our work was for charity concerts, fetes and bazaars.

She would have none of it. 'The Good Lord never meant anyone to earn their living deceiving decent folk with cards and fancies like that.'

'It's not a bad kind of deceiving. No one gets hurt. People deceive themselves and the money goes to charity all the time. Dr Rowe is one of the cleverest men I've ever met, he does a lot of good too. It often helps people to believe in a force outside of themselves – why, only last week he cured two cases of warts.'

'There's only one force outside of us my son, and you'd be best served if you remembered that.'

I was disappointed with Mother's view. But then if I looked back two years to when I'd been a young apprentice lad I suppose the people I was mixing with now would appear a bit strange. She never really objected to my playing the fiddle but of course the company I kept was a different kettle of fish. Perhaps it would be best if I took myself off for a while and had a look around.

I bought myself an old Model-T Ford that cost me twenty-seven pounds, and worth every penny of it. I could stow my fiddle away nicely and keep my clothes neat in a suitcase and my suit always hung up tidily on a hook. There's nothing worse than a shabby appearance and I've never allowed myself to look down at heel even if there's been nothing in my belly. I decided to take a trip and see how far up Australia I could get. I hoped I might reach Cairns if I was lucky. First of all I decided to have a look at Adelaide.

Today it would be impossible for a young man of the same age as I was then to understand the freedom I'd suddenly come by with that old car. When you've always travelled on buses and trains or merely walked then you really appreciate a car.

Adelaide, Sydney, Brisbane, Cairns, they'd all just been names to me before that, but now I had the means to get there and see them. I couldn't have been more thrilled if someone had handed me a magic carpet.

People say Adelaide is very English. If that's the case then I'm not going to bother with England. I reckoned it was a dull sort of place and on the whole I didn't do so well there; not much money and not a very generous class of person at all. I didn't make out very well until I met a useful bloke called Birkenshaw.

This Birkenshaw was an Englishman ... come to think of it, most of the old showfolk were English. They were cool and calculating. He was an escapologist and a sword swallower. He'd get himself chained, tied up and padlocked in a huge box and then be out in under two minutes. He finished his act with sword swallowing and that was what really interested me. I needed something dramatic to finish off my performance, and something like that would set me in a class apart.

Getting down five swords with ease made him a very great attraction at his pitch near the rifle range down at the children's circus on the outskirts of town.

Struggling about inside a box always seems a bit undignified to me and anyhow you need an assistant, but sword swallowing is a different thing altogether. You can do that on your own, and it's a stirring sight.

'Would you teach me?' I asked him. That's quite a thing to ask a showman but I offered good money. He was a master of the art himself but I was sure I could improve upon the act. Admittedly he struggled and groaned a bit and then appeared to force the blade down his gullet but I reckoned I could liven the affair up. Clutch at my stomach, claw at my throat, something to shock the ladies and terrify the kids.

'It'd cost you forty pounds.' That would be a real investment.

'Thirty pounds if I help you with the fiddle.'

The fiddle always attracted a crowd. They would gather round in no time if they heard a few notes of music. His act did not exactly have a dramatic opening, it was more the finale which roused them up. So I considered that if I attracted them in the first place I was an asset.

'See here, I need a helper, you stop with me for a while, there's the fiddling to do and a bit of assisting during the act ... make it thirty-five pounds and we'll shake on it.' So we shook on it.

'Do you usually travel with someone?' I asked.

'I did. But the lazy bitch left me in Port Augusta, took up with a fishmonger.'

I soon realised why. Half the job was keeping him away from the bottle till his act was over. If you kept him off the rum till he was finished, you could let him have the bottle then. A nice drop at the right time seemed to keep him on an even keel. If you let him have his head before the show started then the whole performance went to pot. But if you refused it altogether he got into a very nasty temper.

Sword swallowing isn't easy. I was in the prime of life and even so it took me nearly a month to learn to control my throat muscles. First time off you feel sick as a dog when the steel goes down, then you learn to forget about that and concentrate on the positioning. Throw your head back and open your gullet wide and slide the sword down very slowly, letting it get a bit warm so there's not too much shock to the system.

'Let you have a turn if you get yourself started,' Mr Birkenshaw told me one day. We'd become quite friendly and he appreciated my music which was increasing his audience.

They were quite long, those swords, brilliant and shining and really deadly. Even though they are flexible they can hurt a good deal, but of course the art is in the illusion which must be quite perfect or the effect is spoiled. Soon the first sword was going down a treat but getting the second one down was beyond me. How Mr Birkenshaw swallowed five I just couldn't understand.

By now we had worked out a very slick routine. I'd come on playing 'Loch Lomond' and then he'd follow with his big box.

I'd tie up his legs, strap his hands behind his back and invite anyone from the crowd to come up and inspect my knots and buckles. Then I'd help him into the box, fix a chain round it and fasten the big padlock on the catch.

It took him two minutes to get out ... if he was sober when he went in. Then I'd play another tune and he'd get on with the sword swallowing. When the fifth sword went down the crowd roared and cheered. That would be the finale. He kept telling me that when I'd worked up to a couple of swords I could have a turn, but I felt that such a time would never come.

But events come on a person unexpectedly, and it so happened that one day he got a letter from the lady who had deserted him in Port Augusta, and try as I might I could not keep him off the bottle. He was of a very morose turn of mind when I padlocked him in the box and when I turned to face the crowd to explain how strong he was and what a master of escape I had inside that box, I fairly had to shout to drown the curses coming from him struggling inside.

The crowd didn't care. They stood there all eager and expectant thinking it was part of the act. Then the box began to rock about and terrible thumping sounds were added to his curses and I realised the poor old devil had got in a muddle with his knots.

There was nothing I could do to help him except keep the crowd happy. So I picked up my fiddle and started to play. That didn't work. I had chosen the wrong moment, psychologically speaking, you might say.

'Let him out ... silly old bugger!' the woman at the rifle range shouted. She was jealous of our act, because people always cleared off her pitch quick smart when we got going. That triggered off the crowd and everyone started yelling and cat-calling. It was horrible.

Necessity is the mother of invention. I picked up one of the swords and approached the edge of the stage.

'It is not given to everyone to reveal themselves in a trice,' I shouted and threw my head back and slid the sword down.

There was an immediate hush. The sight of that steel disappearing always got them gasping and luckily the sounds from the box had died down. My oath, I thought, what if he's passed out?

There was nothing for it, I had to delay a little longer so I picked up that second sword. If you've got to accomplish a thing then you can always manage when the important moment comes and the second sword slid down easy and snug with no trouble at all. At that moment I heard the chain fall off the box and I can tell you I never heard a more welcome sound in all my life.

After that night we went on working very successfully for a while. The money was good, the audiences enthusiastic and as time went by I was on to three swords.

We became regulars on that one ground, taking off sometimes to perform at fetes and festivals in the surrounding country. When nothing much was doing we'd hire a church hall in some outlying town and put on a show there. But we always came back to our pitch.

Imagine our annoyance when we got back one Friday to find right next door, so to speak, a fragile-looking old man with a great billboard put up, setting himself out to be 'Professor Wishart – Sword Swallower Extraordinary. Entertainer to the Royalty and Crowned Heads of Europe and The East.'

He was extraordinary all right, being eighty-four and very proud of the fact. Mr Birkenshaw was a kind hearted man, when he was sober. I thought he was very good not taking exception to someone like that just pushing themselves in with such a similar act, right next to us. I think he was sorry for the old man, still working round the shows at his great age. He decided to turn a blind eye to him, relying more on the escapology and my fiddle playing, just putting in the swallowing occasionally.

But it all goes to show you shouldn't let your heart rule your head, even when dealing with the elderly. This Professor Wishart ingratiated himself with everyone and when we'd got used to him he brought out some of the loudest music I've ever heard.

His music drowned my fiddle playing and quite blasted out the patter I gave about Mr Birkenshaw and his box. Added to that he dressed flashly, with glitter trousers and a red cummerbund and a green velvet jacket. He was garish and with his long grey whiskers and rolling eyes, always bloodshot on account of him being so old I suppose, he caught the attention of the crowd more than us. He was one of those people who always had to go one better than anyone else.

Years later I met a snake handler who had the same failing ... always had to go one better. He was bitten by one of his snakes and when they rushed him to hospital he told them it was a taipan. So they gave him the antidote and he promptly died. Stupid man, he'd only been bitten by a grass snake but he thought he'd get into the local papers, get a lot of publicity, if he said he'd been bitten by something deadly. He got into the papers alright, but definitely the wrong column as far as he was concerned.

It was the same with Professor Wishart, always going one better. He swallowed his swords all right but then he topped off the act with a thundering great tent peg. The crowd ooh'd and aah'd with fear in case he'd choke himself ... silly old fool.

'Never mind,' I told Mr Birkenshaw, who was getting depressed at our thinning audience and like everyone who gets depressed, turning his mind back to all the unsatisfactory events they can remember. In his case it was the lady lost in Port Augusta. I could see his thoughts were more and more focussed on the bottle for temporary relief.

'There's more ways of killing a cat than putting salt on its tail ... ' I know that's not quite right but Mother was always saying something like that.

'We're finished Owen,' Mr Birkenshaw kept saying. 'That Wishart's done for us, we'll have to move on permanently.'

'Not on your life, ' I told him. 'When events are going in a negative fashion then you have to look at them in a positive way. No one can defeat you if you act positive.'

Those were not idle words either. To grumble and complain gets you nowhere except saddling you with a bad reputation. You have to be cunning, look around and think your way out of a situation, you have to go one better and beat the other fellow. That was the lesson I learnt the hard way at the YM. You just have to size up the situation and act accordingly ... very swiftly too before the other bloke gets too much of a head start.

The next few days I practised on my own, kept away from everyone, and all the while Wishart's music got louder and louder and our crowd dwindled to a handful. When I felt sure of myself I told Mr Birkenshaw I had a trick that would change our fortunes.

'There's nothing'll get the better of that old goat!'

But he hadn't counted on the power of positive thinking. That evening when the crowd began to collect next door, I waited until Professor Wishart threw his head back. A dreadful ugly sight he was, grey whiskers, scraggy neck and all. When the tent peg was just sliding down I gave a great shout to gain their attention. He couldn't do a thing about it.

'Come and see The Wonder of the Century!' I shouted. 'Come and see The Illuminated Stomach.'

Then I forced my throat open as far as it would go and slid down a narrow electric light bulb while Mr Birkenshaw doused the lights.

How I wish I could have been a fly on the wall! How I wish I could have seen myself. Everyone said my gullet glowed right down to my belly. How they cheered, how they roared! No one had seen anything like it before.

'We're made!' Mr Birkenshaw repeated over and over again. 'Never need to bother now, we can keep going with a fine act like this. We can stay here till after Christmas now.'

But Adelaide didn't hold me any more. The Depression had settled upon us like The Black Death had gripped England centuries ago. After the Wall Street Crash of October 1929, there appeared to be no hope for us over here. Inside a short while one man in three was out of work and many were on the streets trying to find enough to fill their bellies.

Match sellers, religious picture sellers, men selling darning wool and knitting needles, anything to keep themselves going; making their way from town to town, their shoes padded with cardboard and the ache of hunger consuming them. The dole was 5/- a week, a sorry sight they looked in their old dyed army clothing. I could make several pounds a week, there were smart clothes on my back and the old Model-T almost put me in the luxury class. There was a lot to be thankful for.

This was no time to sit in a single place though, just raking over the pickings. Now it would be better to be on the move. After The Crash life would get harder and harder. I should be getting what I could ... where I could.

'You'll learn, like all of 'em you'll learn,' Mr Birkenshaw kept telling me when he knew of my intention. 'Got a good living here ... but you're restless like all young chaps.'

'Seems to me you ought to be looking to the future yourself.

Why not come along with me and we'll travel together?'

'Not on your life. Not me. Setting off in that old rattletrap of yours!'

'I'll be taking it steady going up north.'

'And good luck to you ... bloody silly dingbat.'

As if to prove him right I was no more than a day's journey from Adelaide when the old Model-T broke down. It was not much of a problem but it took me some time, me being out in the blue away from anyone who could lend a hand.

'How yer doin'?' someone called to me, but being under the chassis I couldn't reply very civilly.

The chap who'd spoken was a kindly sort of man, had a little property over the next hill and as dusk was coming on fast he suggested I might like to pull up for the night when I was finished.

'Not much on offer,' he said, a bit shamefaced, when I finally fronted up.

'Cocky's Joy, was all they had. That's boiled wheat and treacle. That was what many families lived on in the country during the hard times.

'Usually there's a bite of rabbit,' his wife explained 'but he's had no luck with the traps today.'

No Luck! As I sat and drank her coffee, a very nice brew too, made from baked wheat put through a mincer, I wonder to myself about this business of luck.

If I wanted to believe there was such a thing as luck then it had certainly been with me so far. When I looked around that poor kitchen, the tea leaves drying on a saucer ready for a second brewing, and the eyes of that man following my every movement in case I brought out some tobacco, and stealing himself for the agony of politely refusing yet hoping against hope I'd insist ... then I knew I must count myself one of the lucky ones

In my heart I didn't believe in luck. Life at first glance appears to be a game of chance, like the throw of a dice, but I was more inclined to believe that life isn't governed by good or bad luck, instead there's more truth in the old saying 'Life is what you make it.'

For that reason I wasn't going to sit down in Adelaide and just take what life handed out to me. I was going off to see what I could do for myself.

When I sat on that first pavement in Geelong I had nothing to lose. If no one had flung their money down then I could have gone home with my tail between my legs and joined the queue with Dad. Now I had everything to lose. The old Model-T, my fiddle and my nice suit. I'd come a long way and it wasn't luck that had been at my elbow, it had been self-confidence. Not enough to make me cocky, but just enough to keep me ticking over nicely.

There are some people who can be born with every advantage under the sun, but if some chance of their upbringing has robbed them of their belief in themselves they'll never set the pond on fire. Whereas you can come across someone who's not even had a decent shirt on their back but was started off in some happy, carefree fashion by their old mum and dad, and they have this wonderful feeling of confidence. There's no holding them.

Fed at the breast with self-confidence, then weaned on to positive thinking. That's my recipe for bringing up any child. Unbeatable. That's what gives people the ability to turn disaster into triumph – positive thinking, not just luck.

Take the Handless Wonder, for instance. He really was a wonder, being able to tie his shoelaces, write a letter and draw a picture, all using his stumps.

'Lost them in the chaff cutter when I was a lad,' he explained. 'Best day's work I ever did. None of my brothers have had a full day's work these two years gone, but I've never wanted – and I've got plenty in the bank.'

There! That's what I mean! Positive thinking at its best.

Chapter 4

Not So Good

'Come here pup!' I was sitting playing the fiddle in the park near Central Station in Sydney when I first noticed the little pup sitting watching me. Only when some kids ran by and kicked a stone at him had he shifted. He slunk into the bushes, his eyes still fixed on me.

'C'mon ... have a bit of pie. Teatime, c'mon, have a piece of pie.' His skinny body shrank further into the shade of the undergrowth.

I sat and watched him and he watched the pie. A pigeon bustled over and as she bobbed her way towards the lump of pastry he lunged for it and the bird squawked off.

'Want another bit?' But he'd slipped back under the bushes.

Not only dogs were starving, whole families were coming to grips with poverty throughout the country.

Poverty has two faces. No one minds being poor if they've got something to look forward to. You can live on the sniff of an oil rag if you've got hope ... can see a job ahead. Many a time I've started off the day with an empty pocket and by the evening had my bag full of money. The other face of poverty, when you can't see any hope of a job and nothing improving, is degrading and grinds you down.

'Susso!' I'd heard the schoolkids calling out of the trains back in Melbourne.

'Susso!' they yelled at the men working on the track, and all the while sniggering to themselves. How could kids understand the feelings of those blokes on sustenance? I thanked my lucky stars I wasn't one of them.

'C'mon pup,' I tried again with the dog. He put his head on one side and for a brief second the tip of his tail moved. Like the shadow of a smile.

'Here ... take this,' he crept out again and had another piece of pie. I stretched down to pat him and straight away he was flat on his belly. Although he was cowed he didn't pull back as I ran my fingers through his silky black and white coat. In spite of his bony condition his coat was soft, his eyes bright and his paws broad and strong.

'Kicked out on the streets old boy?' He rolled over and paddled his legs in the air, the burden of filling his empty stomach forgotten for one puppyhood moment. Squirming on his back he urged me to scratch his belly, but some people walked by and he leapt up and bounded for the bushes again.

When I'd earned a few bob I packed up the fiddle and started off for the car but hadn't reached the edge of the park when I found the dog right by my heels.

'Here ... you go back, pup,' I told him, really fierce. I didn't want to be lumbered with an animal; it took enough to keep myself going.

He sat down and waited till I'd gone a few feet then he was right behind me again. That dog must have had some Blue Heeler in him, he might as well have been tied to my ankle by an invisible string. When I got to the pavement and was about to cross the road he was still there.

Shout and shake my fist as I might he wouldn't shift. He just stood there looking at me with those keen brown eyes, as if he was saying 'There's nowhere else in the world for me to go, so I'm coming along with you.'

And that's how I came by young Masher (I called him that on account of his success with the ladies). He was the first dog I ever owned and the very best too. Quick as a flash he was, always at my heels, never strayed for an instant. Although he was a small dog he had the most fearsome growl. His growl rumbled up from somewhere deep inside and if anyone approached the car or me once it was dark he kept them at bay with a real menacing display. Hackles up, teeth bared, he gave them fair warning. He was a first-rate guard.

Animals are one of life's gifts; there's more pleasure to be had from the companionship of a nice little dog or a chimp or the birds than from many a yacking woman or mate most times.

With Masher on the seat beside me I headed off up north again. I travelled to Newcastle, Taree, Kempsey, Coffs Harbour, and way up into Queensland. All foreign territory to me.

If money had been scarce down south it was practically nonexistent around the towns north of Brisbane during the Depression. People lived from hand to mouth and bartering replaced the passing of money. What had I to barter? Only my fiddle playing, and people can do without that when their bellies are empty, so I soon began to feel the draught.

'Coupla days I'll give yer,' the owner of a cane plantation near Proserpine told me when desperation turned me in search of some work to keep me on the road.

Cane cutting is backbreaking, exhausting work under the sizzling sun. I've heard Queensland is the nearest land in the world to the equator that employs white labour. And did we labour! From sun up to sun down the sweat poured off me so constantly I wondered it hadn't worn a groove in my forehead.

One night, I was bringing the cart back on its final run when something the size of a rabbit but white like a cat darted from the standing cane. The ponies took fright and were off. One moment I'd been walking at their side and the next second my leg was twisted up in a loose rope end which was hanging down from the load. I was dragged nearly fifty yards, and the harder the ponies strained the tighter the rope pulled around my leg. When I finally rolled free they careered off up the track leaving me a twisted heap of numbness.

Masher never left my side. He licked my face and whined and when some bloke ran up he snarled and stood over me with such defiance that they had to toss a sack over him before they could get at me.

Laid out on the floor of one of the huts, I was sure that this was going to be my final resting place. The pain in my back was such that I was certain I'd smashed my spine. But the others reckoned I'd just wrenched myself badly, and anyhow, it was no good thinking otherwise because how could I afford a doctor?

For the next week I lay on that beaten earth floor, staring at the broiling tin roof each day, sweat running down me and my back pierced with such thrusts of pain that deep down I was beginning to despair I'd ever be up and on my two feet and living my old life.

'Buggered yerself up real good!' cackled one of the old timers. 'Lucky bastard though, last year one bloke got both his bloody legs chopped off, right above the knee ... full cart run right over them it did. You should have heard him holler! Reckon you ought to be thanking your bloody stars 'stead of gawking up at the roof like that and feeling sorry for yerself.'

'How'm I ever going to sit behind that wheel of mine again?'

'Fix yerself up a bloody backrest ... keep yerself upright ... you'll be right.'

Ten days passed before I could creep out of that hut and get over to the car. The old bloke had been right, with a bit of fitting and padding with some rags I made myself a backrest and shook off the dust of that dreadful place. Even if every bump in the road twisted the raw nerves in my back at least I was on the move again.

*   *   *

A hint of menace snatched at my heels. Only four days later I was camped one night on the banks of a creek when I heard voices below. Only a while back I'd have walked down to pass the time of day but that painful blow struck by Fate had damaged my self confidence as well as my back. I did not feel as sure of life as I'd always been. After dousing the fire and putting Masher on a piece of rope I turned in for the night.

A tremendous thump woke me. Dawn had barely come and with the thud still echoing in my ears I was sure a storm had broken overhead. But there was no rain and when I looked up the sky was clear of clouds.

I crept to the edge of the bank and looked down. The river was a mass of swirling rubbish, slimy branches thrown up from the depths and swathes of weed spinning across the surface. Scrambling down the bank opposite came a horde of Italians, leaping into the water and snatching up the dead fish floating amongst the flotsam.

Dynamiting! An ignorant, wasteful method of getting fish. Killing off the young ones and ruining the breeding grounds just to pull a few big ones out of the water.

'We'll get going,' I told the dog. 'Further from home the rougher it seems to get.'

Back on the road it was good to feel the miles ticking up again but nothing was set fair for that trip. Crossing the O'Connell

River I nearly lost the Model-T due to the cunning wickedness of the old man who lived in a humpy near the track. When I drove down to the crossing I could see the river bed was a bit muddy, but there were no more than a few inches of water and I should have no trouble getting across.

'How yer doin' mate?' I called to the old bloke who was sitting up on the bank picking his teeth with a bit of straw.

'Good,' was all he said, yawning and scratching himself.

I got into low gear and started across. Only a third of the way over, the offside wheels sank deep in mud. The sand and mud overlaying the crossing had been so churned up I'd strayed into a pothole. Nothing would shift that car. One side was down and she sat there like a lump of lead.

'Thirty bob a tow!' The old boy yelled from the bank.

'Go to buggery!' I saw red. I'd only got four pounds in the world.

'Tide's on the turn.'

That did it. I'd not realised the river was tidal in these parts. Cursing and swearing to myself I waded back and handed him the thirty shillings and out from behind his humpy he drove a pair of horses, already harnessed. He dragged the car out to the other side smooth as clockwork, unhitched, turned the horses, slapped their rumps and went back across the river making sure they muddied up the edge of the crossing. I reckon he'd got himself an income for life.

There was next to no money coming in and after a couple of weeks up there, trying my luck round the hotels and the high streets, I decided to head for home, taking a different route, travelling further inland.

Not having a very clear idea of the roads I went in a general southerly direction. The weather was settled but very hot and although my back was still painful my spirits rose as I began to put the miles behind me. Getting fed up with the dusty main roads I decided to branch off onto a smaller track. After all I was still travelling south, and I could do without the traffic.

My spirits continued to rise and I whistled a little tune to myself. Even facing in the direction of home gave me a really good feeling inside. It was too good, really. I wasn't concentrating properly and next thing as I turned a sharp bend the car lurched in to a dried out gully where the last rains had sliced a narrow, deep path across the track. When I revved she only settled back with a loud bang and stopped there like a wounded creature. I'd done the crankshaft.

This whole trip was dogged by bad luck! I could have sat there and cursed all the powers of Heaven and Hell which had landed me in this fix, but I knew I had only myself to blame. Careering along without one thought in my head except to leave the dust of that part of the world behind me.

Cars! Lonely tracks! Grasping locals! No money, my back playing up, no work, no nothing ... if I lost that car then I'd really had it. True, I'd get myself back to Melbourne somehow or another, but my old Model-T was my home and my refuge as well as my transport. That car was the best thing I'd ever owned, and now it was lying useless in that dry creek through my own carelessness. Matters had never seemed more desperate and my mind was quite clouded over with despair. So clouded with despair, in fact, that it was quite a while before I could believe the evidence of my own eyes. Lying in the bush, half covered with a trailing creeper and canted over at an undignified angle was another Model-T. I was not the only one who'd come to grief on that sharp bend.

I stared stupidly at the old wreck, not thinking properly, not using my brain, still sunk in my own misery. Masher began to sniff about in the undergrowth but I called him away. There'd been several snakes on the track as I'd driven along, so I shut him in the car and carefully circled the abandoned Model-T.

A thicket of lantana sprouted up through the gaping window spaces and a sapling struggled to push through the gap between the running board and the car. All the wheels had been taken years ago, the upholstery had vanished and a lizard slid away inside the exhaust pipe. The only part of that car which was not ruined was the crankshaft. Not impossible. Only very nearly impossible!

The difficulties were almost too great to think of. No help, no tools to speak of and hardly any food or water. The main worry was the snakes. Even as I sat there I'd watched a deaf adder moving along the crazed surface of the dried out mud in the creek bed. Whatever I did I'd have to make sure I moved very carefully, because the kind of mistake I might make wouldn't give me a second chance.

'Nothing for it old mate,' I shouted to the dog, 'this is where we get our hands dirty.'

Still leaving Masher in the car I found myself a stout stick and systematically beat down all the undergrowth around the old wreck.

What slithered and slipped out of that lot made my hair stand on end. I reckon I'd landed in the happy hunting ground for all snakes north of Brisbane. But snakes, like most animals, are more eager to get out of your way than pick a fight. The only real worry were the deaf adders. They truly don't hear you and they're deadly. You can put your foot on them and that can be a nasty experience for man or beast.

As I was thrashing away at the scrub a young lad came round the bend. He stood there, just stood and watched. He was not a pure-bred Aborigine; he had a bit of European blood. His forehead was unusually large and prominent, his face heavy and his eyes just everywhere and yet nowhere.

'How yer goin' mate!' I shouted. He stood there watching, still silent.

'Got meself in a proper fix ... can yer lend a hand?' He still stood there and I could almost see the words ticking through that huge, oversized head and the thoughts turning over. Should he show a clean pair of heels or should he stop?

He still said nothing. He didn't smile, didn't frown, but he didn't make off either. Maybe it was a fancy of mine but I sensed he was listening. His head was slightly cocked on one side and once or twice he glanced up the track behind him.

'Worth a quid or two to you.' At that he nodded and came down into the bed of the creek.

'What's yer name?'

'Sadly.'

'Sadly?'

I'd expected a Billy or a Jim. Anything but 'Sadly'. Perhaps that huge head had something to do with it.

One thing for sure, he'd never be dux of the school for conversation. I'd never met such a silent lad, and as we worked together I reckoned I addressed more remarks to the dog than to him.

I'll give him his due, though. He worked all right. He tore at the undergrowth and shifted boulders like one possessed. I fancied he was as eager to see that car on the road as I was.

'Two days I reckon this'll take us if we work solid.' I told him. He said nothing.

'Can you find me some water?' He shook his head firmly and turned his back on me. 'Isn't there a property ahead up the track?'

He shrugged but didn't turn round. Soon the car was stripped of every bit of greenery and I could crawl underneath and see how to start about getting the crank out.

'Give us a hand,' I yelled. 'Fetch that box out of the boot. I'll need me tools.' There was no reply. When I turned round he was standing by the edge of the track, head slightly on one side, listening.

'Come on, if anyone comes you'll know all right. Come on.' I shouted. The job was difficult enough without any half-baked kid like him standing around dreaming.

Those Model-Ts had a thing or two over our modern cars. If you should ever need to take the crank out of one of these smart up-to-date jobs you'd have to lift the engine out and Heaven knows what. The old Model-T was a dream by comparison. You can get the crank out with very little trouble from underneath. True, in this case there were other problems. Every nut and bolt had been rusted in solid so I had to cut my way through with hammer and chisel, but it wasn't an impossible job.

Battering and hammering away trying to get the flywheel off I wasn't giving a thought to anything else in the world and when I eased myself out to fish for a piece of rag to wipe my brow I was stunned to find two men standing right over me.

They were staring at me long and hard from under their widebrimmed hats. Their horses were champing the grass on the top of the bank. They must have slipped down and been standing there for some time. I glanced around for the boy but there was no sign of him.

'Private property mate!'

'Git goin', the taller of the two said, and flicked his whip at the bonnet of the abandoned car.

'Now wait on ... I took a wrong turning, my oath I did. Look what it's landed me into.'

'Git goin,' he repeated.

'Yer seen a young Abo? Crazy kid,' the other asked, ignoring his mate.

'Not seen no one, 'cepting yerselves.' I fancied I caught the flicker of movement from under my chassis.

'He's that bloody stupid he'll be on the track somewhere. He'd be too scared to go far.'

'Yeah, silly as a wet hen.'

'He'll be around. Look, we're on to this stupid bastard. If you see him keep him, we'll be back.'

'And you'd better be finished next time we're round.'

'We'll be back tomorrow.' With that they clambered up the bank to their horses, wheeled them round and were off.

'Phew ... what was all that about?' I called under the car and shook the lad's leg. But he wouldn't come out. He stopped there still as a log for ten minutes after they'd left and then inched out very cautiously.

'What you done? What they want you for?'

He shook his head and turned his back. There was not much point persisting, and what was the use of poking my nose into another's business? I let the matter drop.

'You did all right,' I told him that night as we sat by the fire. The bush was silent, not another human being had passed along the track and barely three words had we exchanged as we worked together. It was a pleasure to even hear my own voice.

The crank was now out of the old car; the pistons had been rusted in but I managed to take the crank out leaving them behind. I'd nearly finished removing the broken crank from my own car. We'd got on well with the job.

'Comin' along of you,' he suddenly said.

I shook my head. I needed no company, not another mouth to feed. I wanted no responsibilities.

'This is your place, you should stop here,' I told him. 'Young lad like you shouldn't wander off from home. What about your mum?'

' 'Ain't got no mum.'

'Well, yer dad.' He said nothing.

'Anyhow, about those men. What'd they want you for?'

'See'd 'em I did.'

'What you seen?'

That pudding-faced lad put his hands over his eyes and sunk his head on his chest as though he would wipe out for ever what it was he had seen. Masher sidled over and licked the boy's hands.

' 'ere come on ... can't be that bad. Tell us what you've seen.'

But he shook his head and said nothing.

'I can't take someone along of me if I don't know nothing about them.'

That did it. He stared into the flames for a long time as he considered, one hand fondling the dog's ears. Finally he made up his mind and looked me in the eyes. Straight in the eyes.

' 'e was dragged. Round and round they dragged him.'

'Who?'

'Me dad. He said they had a skinful. "Keep away from 'em" he told me, and we ran, but they caught him. Tied him to their truck and set off 'cross the paddock.'

'Those men? You mean they tied him up and just took off?'

He nodded.

'When did this happen?'

Try as I might he'd not say another word.

Drunk? Bored? Restless? They'd be back looking for the only witness. Chances were they weren't that stupid that they wouldn't see I'd had some help with all that work.

'Turn in,' I told him. 'We'll need an early start.'

Up before dawn we worked like creatures possessed. Heaving, struggling, fumbling and forcing we toiled under the car all morning. Between us we propped up each end of the crank with rocks and pieces of wood, and finally we offered it up for its final positioning. No chance of fitting the bearings; there was nothing sophisticated about the job I did.

When I gently eased the old car out of the gully there were some troublesome knocks but she kept going. Not thinking, I continued back down the track trying to make up my mind how serious those knocking bearings were, then I heard a desperate cry behind me.

That Sadly was haring along behind me as if his life depended on keeping up.

'Give us a break ... I'd got to come back for the gear,' I grumbled. 'I was only trying her out.'

He flung himself into the back seat and nothing would shift that boy till we'd travelled twenty miles or more.

Sadly stayed with me for three days. I reckon he felt by then he'd put enough space between himself and those two.

What had really happened back there in the bush to him and

his father? Had something that started as a thoughtless lark ended up with real tragedy? Would they go on searching for the only witness? Sitting by the fire that night I found myself constantly peering into the shadows and when I'd turned in the least movement from young Masher wrenched me from my fitful sleep.

Enormous men, giant-like, without brains, their massive hands outstretched, stalked me through the desolate landscape of my dreams, while hollow-eyed women watched and waited for my bones to be brought to the graveyard of their hopes, where skulls and vertebrae rattled amongst heaps of broken cartwheels, rusted engines and rotting floorboards.

I must get back home, back to where I understood the people and their ways. Leave the heat and the dust and the crudity of this part of the world behind me.

Life was too cheap up here, Death must knock at their miserable doors like a long-awaited friend. I wanted none of it. I wanted to feel alive again, not just a downtrodden morsel of humanity.

Chapter 5

The Brown Bird

A couple of mornings later I was driving along with the dust rising up like a great cloud behind me when I saw a movement on the road immediately ahead. There, fluttering in the dust, was a fair-sized brown bird. I'll never know what kind of a bird it was. It was more like a very large finch than anything else, with a straight beak, not curved like a bird of prey.

Flight was obviously impossible, so it just sat on the palm of my hand and stared at me with that beady look birds have. There's something desperate about an injured creature, or for that matter, any animal that is in your power. They sit there with a helpless resignation as though they know that with one flick of your wrist you could snap their necks. They can't cringe or beg, they just have to sit there and take it.

Years later I took over a chimpanzee in a menagerie attached to a circus. This chimp had a nasty temper, and the owners only tolerated her because she was such a great attraction. If people were foolish enough to put their hands through the bars then it was their lookout.

There was a lion tamer with that circus, hoping to marry the owner's daughter. He was a great show-off of a bloke who liked to make the chimp mad by poking sticks at her and snatching his hand away just before she got her teeth in.

One day he moved a bit too slowly and she had a mouthful of him. Did he holler! He swore she was a danger to everyone around and would be taking the hand off someone before long, and went straight off to get his revolver and finish her off then and there. You could tell he was making a big thing out of it and would look pretty heroic in that young woman's eyes when he swaggered in and shot the poor chimp.

Realisation dawned in that animal's eyes, she knew something was up. She turned around, shut her eyes tight and sat huddled in the corner of the cage. The sight of her was horrifying, as if she'd been a human being.

'Give that to me,' I told the man when he returned with the gun. 'I'll change her ways.'

'Let me go in there,' I asked the owner, reckoning he didn't really want to lose a valuable animal.

'I'll finish the bloody monster off!' yelled the lion tamer. But the owner took the gun from him and told me to get in the cage.

I went in to her, no rope, no chain in my hand. I just talked to her.

'It's like this,' I said. 'You may think we're a poor, pale-faced, smelly bunch of creatures from where you're sitting, but who pays for your bananas and your oranges? Who cares for you? Is it right to bite the hand that feeds?'

I sat in front of that chimp and very gently touched her furry arm and I swear she hid her head in shame. She never touched me and she never went for anyone else while I was in that circus.

The bird sat on my hand and didn't budge an inch. I've always loved birds ever since those days when I spent my Saturdays at the racecourse.

She was a pretty thing. I put her on the seat of the car and she didn't move, just sat there waiting to see what would happen. As we were at midday I decided I might as well stay put and have a bite to eat. She'd probably fly off in a few minutes. I guessed she'd only been knocked a bit silly by a flying stone from some passing car.

'Don't you sing?' I asked, she peered at me very knowingly. I took out my fiddle and settled down on the running board.

'How'd you like 'Loch Lomond'?'

Before I'd played more than a few bars that bird stood up, stretched her neck and flapped her wings. Then she settled back again with her head on one side and listened. Half the world would have had me shut up, locked away in a safe place, if they'd seen me sitting out there on that dusty road playing to a strange bird.

'You looking for a perch?' I asked and edged the bow over to her. I touched her claws, and quick as a flash she hopped onto the bow and sat there as if she'd been accustomed to a fiddler's bow all her life. Must have thought a suitable twig had come her way just for convenience.

That bird showed me where my way lay during the weeks ahead. Soon she would sit on my bow all the while I played my tunes and in no time at all I was drawing people quicker than ever before.

'Look at that bird!' they'd cry, and the pennies and the threepenny bits and sixpences would roll in faster than ever.

I could not explain to this day why I can communicate with birds. There is something in the fiddle that strikes a chord in them. The quarter tones are the notes that do it. As soon as I played those quarter tones the birds cocked their heads on the side and I found that if wanted them to follow my wishes I merely had to concentrate on them. First of all I only had the little brown one, but later hundreds of different birds passed through my hands and rarely did I find one that did not respond. They would turn around, on the command. They would stand to attention, sometimes I could train them to act dead. Just tell them they were dead birds, play a few sombre chords, and they'd flop down. Communication was not difficult and all their tricks were very simple. I've never been able to stand those acts where birds put on a real show of roller skating and pulling tiny chariots and the like. That's not natural at all.

Desolation lifted and instead of looking at my fellow men with suspicion in my heart I regarded them more kindly once again. I'd come down from the north with a sick and bitter view of life, but each day was becoming a little better than the next. The burden of depression was lifting.

But the heat was still there, day after day burnt itself out under a cruel blue sky until I felt the very world was about to set itself afire and the branches of the gums cracked and crackled overhead, tense and eager for the flames. By the time I reached northern New South Wales the days were still so hot that the sweat ran down my back as I drove, and by night my body was desiccated.

'Mate of yours in the sleep-out,' I'd stopped at a country hotel and the publican was chatting as he wiped over the counter.

'Mate of mine?' That was impossible. All my mates were in Melbourne.

'Birdman, like you. Though he hasn't got a fiddle. Still he's got birds all right, not just one like you. He's got a whole cageful, poor old bugger.'

'What's up?'

'On his way out, I reckon.'

I found the birdman lying on a wooden stretcher in the sleep-out, his face turned to the wall and sweat standing out on his forehead. Several weeks of white stubble frosted his chin and his breath came in painful gulps.

'How yer goin' mate?' A stupid sort of question for me to ask really. I guessed the landlord hadn't been far out with his opinion, but you have to say something after all.

The old man didn't reply. He turned to look at me but even then I think he was only turning in the direction of my voice. He'd gone too far for his eyes to focus properly. Blue edges encircled the black pupils of his eyes, those mauvey blue rims you see in the eyes of the very sick.

'Reckoned he was flat broke when he landed up here,' the publican called through the doorway. The man rolled his head from side to side as though trying to shut out the other man's words.

'But he's lucky. The Salvos are picking him up after tea and they'll look after him. See how he goes from there. You'll be right, mate!' he added with an easygoing cackle.

The publican was a kind hearted man even if he was a bit casual towards the old chap. I've known many who wouldn't let a dying man stop under their roof. Bad for trade, they'd say.

Dying on your own is a cruel business. The best I could do, I figured, was to sit with him for a while. His eyes were closed when I went back after eating my tea. As I pulled up an old box and sat down, his lips were moving but no sound came out, and all the while his bony mottled fingers picked ceaselessly at the sheets as though impatient to be off. Then all of a sudden he strained himself up and his eyes opened wide as if he'd remembered something very important. He rolled his head from side to side, frowning with anxiety.

'What's up old mate?' I asked, and he stretched out one arm, pointing towards the end of the room.

Down by the door was a square shape covered with a chenille tablecloth. He pointed desperately and muttered to himself.

Two rows of little black eyes peered at me when I took the cloth away. The cage was full of birds. Budgies, lorikeets, rosellas; a couple of dozen birds all squeezed in together with scarcely room to move. The floor of the cage was filthy, the seedpots were empty and the water dish bone dry.

'Them's the birds,' called the landlord as he came past the door. 'Reckon that's why he's hung on so long, keeping going because of them birds. He's got some sort of act, regular bird-man, been up this way many a time. I've told him, if he can't afford the food for them he'd best let them go, but he says they'll be butchered by the wild birds and those that ain't butchered'll starve to death. Never having had to fend for themselves.

'But he's past working with the birds now, and that's for sure. The Salvos won't take them and that's for sure too. Cost a fortune in seed, they would.'

'I'll take them,' I said, and I swear there was the shadow of a grin on that old face. 'Give you something for them mate,' I whispered close to his ear, not wanting the landlord to know I was handing the bloke anything on account of him probably owing the man a packet ... anyhow I didn't feel easy taking advantage of a dying man.

He understood all right, shook his head most definitely when I reached for my pocket. He grabbed my arm and pointed to the birds nodding his head quite excited. 'They're starvin', he managed to say.

Those were the only words he spoke and it's strange when you come to think of it. He was the man who really set me on my feet and yet he spoke only those two words.

As soon as I got those birds in the back of my car the little wild one flew off and I never saw her again. I'd have given all of them away again for the sight of her just once more. Still, perhaps she was sent as a sign, a pointer along the way so to speak, to tell me how my life should be led.

Once fed and housed in more roomy cages than their single old cramped one, those birds gave of their best. My music had the same effect upon them as it had on the wild bird when I found her. They'd sit upon my bow, march up and down and altogether make a very pretty setting for my fiddle playing.

Chapter 6

The Violin Factory

'About time you were back,' Dr Rowe told me as soon as I reached Melbourne. 'More work than I can handle at the moment. Charity's a very popular thing these days among the upper class.'

'We consider you an embellishment,' Mora told me very kindly, kindly for her, that is.

They relied on me to focus the attention of their audience. Stands to reason when a hostess has got a garden full of ladies and gentlemen strolling among the shrubs and gossiping, you can't expect her to go bellowing through the flower beds to get them to come and listen to the entertainment. Once I sat down and started to play people always drifted over and then the act could begin more naturally.

The only fly in the ointment was that Mora did not like birds. In fact she could not have picked up a little bird to save her life. She reckoned she was allergic to feathers. Birds terrified her.

'Perhaps you were an insect in your previous life?' I suggested, but seeing her nasty look I made it sound a bit nicer. 'I can imagine you as a lovely butterfly, mark my words, that's why you have this revulsion, this dreadful instinct to fly from them.'

That put her right again. You had to be a bit careful with Mora, she had a nasty tongue in her mouth if she liked. Same as with Dr Rowe, who could make you feel that small you wanted to slide under the door.

I remember one particular garden party when we were performing at Lady Argyle's house in Toorak. Sir Stanley Argyle was an important politician of his day. I'd fairly got the crowd eating out of my hand, having played a couple of tunes, swallowed four swords and then taken the little birds from their cage. The birds had marched and waltzed and sat upon my bow as I played. The crowd was nicely warmed up for the doctor but they wouldn't let me go.

'Encore!' they kept shouting, very upper class. So I gave one encore and still they shouted so I gave them another. I could see the Doctor beginning to fidget behind our screen.

Lady Argyle came up, a fine figure of a woman, dressed in white with lace all down the front of her blouse and a diamond as big as a bean on her finger.

'How do you train those charming little birds, Mr Lloyd?' she asked. I said it was not a myth but a reality, and that those little birds were actuated by the Spirit of the Unknown same as we are. It was not trickery she had witnessed but a demonstration of the power of the mind.

'It's the birdseed,' the Doctor called from behind the screen. 'It's something he puts in the birdseed,' and he gave a really nasty, sarcastic laugh.

But Lady Argyle turned her back on him. She knew. She was a clever woman ... and a real lady too. She understood more than the Doctor about the little birds.

Dr Richard Rowe had been boss cocky wherever he'd performed and you didn't have to be a mind reader to tell I was becoming more of a rival than an attraction. For my own part I'd become used to being my own master and didn't take too kindly to his condescending ways.

Being of this frame of mind I happened to fall into conversation with an Italian bloke in Collins Street. He played the flute. In company with another chap with a guitar and a third on the mandolin they were out in all weathers, come rain or shine. When gusts of wind whipped along the gutters they'd shelter in the doorways of the larger buildings until the police shifted them along.

They were a cut above me, mainly on account of their superior repertoire. People would come up and ask for a tune and nine times out of ten they'd play it straight off. Whether it was 'The Indian Love Call' or 'The Golliwogs' Cakewalk' or 'Toselli's Serenade', they never faltered. Faultless they were, whereas if anyone asked me for anything more up to date than 'The Skye Boat Song' I was in a proper fix and had to act a bit deaf.

'Do a bit of the same sort of thing meself,' I volunteered one day as I stood and watched them. They didn't look at me.

'Think there might be something in it for me?' I went on.

'You think?' one of them snapped in a very discouraging tone.

'I've been out with my fiddle a few years now,' I told them.

'Times are hard,' was the only answer I got.

'You haven't got a fiddle here.' I decided to attack with a positive statement of fact.

'Forget it,' I was told.

But I didn't feel like forgetting it. I wanted to get myself more up to date. The public was becoming more sophisticated, I needed a touch of the romantic, a bit of syncopation, a dash of the classical, in fact I needed to get abreast of the times.

'If you don't ask you don't get' is a very true saying, and if you want to find something then you're best going to those who really know their art instead of messing around on your own. It saves a lot of time and trouble. I'd made up my mind those Italians could teach me a lot.

As I persisted they began arguing among themselves and because they couldn't get rid of me they agreed in the end that I could go back with them that night and meet their mate, Philli, who was very interested in all kinds of musicians.

Philli was not just a musician though, he was a craftsman. He ran The Violin Factory at Leighton Street in Carlton. Violins dominated the place but besides them there were harps, guitars, cellos, banjos – every stringed instrument you could call to mind.

Stepping into The Violin Factory took you straight into another world. Philli sat at the back of the shop near his workbench and in the other corner the stove glowed day and night, with the coffee pot always on it. In that dark room he worked, ate, slept and talked from morning to night. Music flowed in his veins the same as blood did in ordinary folk.

'You'll have to listen carefully,' Philli told me when I'd explained that I'd like to join them. 'To learn you have to be prepared to listen, remember that.' He looked at my fiddle but he didn't say much. From the way he held it I knew he didn't appreciate the workmanship.

'First let me listen to you.'

I started off with 'Loch Lomond', then 'Annie Laurie' and I finished with a jig I was very fond of playing. From the expression in his eyes his opinion was not approving.

'Would you like to listen to this?' he asked and picked up a violin, the likes of which I'd never seen before in all my life.

The wood was glowing and honey coloured; one side was intricately inlaid with different woods depicting a scene in a European city – Italy I suppose. Tiny houses, little churches with pointed roofs and a castle towering over them all, not a lick of paint in the whole picture, all done with neatly fitted strips of wood. The instrument was a work of art in itself, not counting the sound that came from it.

Inlaid all around the side of the fiddle was a sentence. 'Viva est in silva,' it said.

'What's that?'

'Life is in the wood. It is Latin. Life is in the wood.'

And that was true. The wood of that instrument spoke to me. The sounds rose and swelled and filled The Violin Factory. As his bow swept across the strings they spoke of love and death, dreadful sadness and sorrow and then great happiness. The whole of life spun around that little man playing the violin. He was more a magician than anyone I've ever met.

'You like my music?' He looked at me with laughter in his eyes.

'It's magic.'

'You are one of us, I would say. Not everyone can learn, but you will.'

Several troupes of musicians made The Violin Factory their home. Up above the workshop was a second and third floor honeycombed with passages and tiny rooms. Most times everyone paid their way but if a poor patch came Philli didn't press them for anything. If there wasn't a bed to spare then they could settle down in a corner of the workshop. No musician was ever turned away.

When there was money in their pockets they shared it around at The Violin Factory. They'd start coming in at dusk, bread tucked under their arms, perhaps even a bottle of wine in their hands or sausages filling their pockets. You were either up or down at The Violin Factory. You tasted life to the full. Cut out the greys and dull browns. You looked only at the black and the white of life and threw yourself into its pleasure and pain.

Philli's cooking was the beginning of an evening of joy. Once the light of day had gone he'd down his tools. Daylight was the only light for working by, he reckoned. He'd clear up his bench and then tie a huge white apron round his middle. The coffee pot would be refilled with water and after grinding a fresh pile of beans he sat and smoked and thought about the evening meal. Philli was a wonderful cook.

He was an artist in all he did. If he hadn't been a prime violin maker then he'd have been a Cordon Bleu chef ... no doubt about it. Never before or since have I tasted pizzas like his or spaghetti with sauce just like the sauce he made.

His speciality was a dish we all called Stuffed Noodles. 'Lasagne Imbottite', he corrected our ignorance. Lovingly he'd boil the lasagne and chop the celery and grate the cheese, all the time whistling and singing to himself. As he laid the layers of cheese, noodle and sausage one on top of the other and poured the thick red tomato sauce over the lot, topping off with a final layer of cheese, we'd watch him with such hunger gnawing away inside us that we didn't know how we'd manage the half hour or so till it was on the table. No one went hungry at Philli's even if some days there was no more than cold sausage and a few slices of bread. No one was ever turned away.

Besides Philli, the Violin Factory was part owned by Louis Padula, a harpist who owned a magnificent gilt framed harp which had been brought over on a sailing ship fifty years ago. He spoke of the harp as though it was a gracious traveller, just stopping over in our crude country for a few years. Louis and Philli did not regard instruments merely as objects. To them they had personalities, histories and futures worth bothering about.

Louis reckoned I needed a completely new repertoire before I could get anywhere in their world.

'You are old fashioned,' he told me straight, and tossed over a sheet of music.

'No good to me,' I had to admit. 'Can't read a note.' His eyebrows shot up and his mouth drooped. I don't think he'd imagined anyone could be as ignorant as that.

And so I got down to learning their kind of music. Sitting listening to them playing, joining in with the simplest melodies to begin with and then practising them on my own. There wasn't another place in the whole world where I could have learnt so quickly.

As soon as darkness fell the musicians started arriving in their twos and threes. No matter how long they'd stood on street corners, nor how many miles they'd wandered with their instruments, once inside the old Violin Factory they were refreshed. Maybe it was the smell of the spaghetti or the minestrone or the lasagne or the taste of the rough red wine which breathed new life into them, or perhaps it was the sound of Philli's violin as he stood and played in the shadows of that enormous room.

Aria, waltz, mazurka and lullaby mingled with the scent of coffee and tobacco to produce a magic potion that turned dreams into substance. One by one the others would take up their instruments and follow his lead. Il Trovatore, Carmen, Tosca, Toselli's Serenade, The Turkish Patrol, La Paloma ... the room shook and trembled as flute, cello, harp, guitar, mandolin and fiddle followed his lead.

Where he led they followed and music lived and breathed under those rough beams. Music came alive in that cavernous place where the walls were hung with tools and instruments, where the rain sometimes blew through the cracks in the window and the mice scuttled under the workbench searching for crumbs.

Ever since those days I've been unable to sit in a concert hall or a theatre and watch someone performing on a stage with any feeling of pleasure at all. They give me the same feeling as seeing a young tree or shrub planted in a tub inside of those glass and metal skyscrapers in the city. Divorced from reality. I've seen music, I've felt music, I've eaten, drunk and slept music and there's no comparison.

Soon I'd picked up enough of their tunes to go out with some of the lads. Being with other musicians was a new experience, not so lucrative, of course, so I still kept to my own activities with the little birds and the Rowes. We were a good group. There was Lindsay with his guitar, Professor Foley Westwood who'd once played with the Jacobean Quartet but had fallen on hard times, and then we had a blind chap we had to lead everywhere, who'd lost his sight from a bout of syphilis when only a young fellow.

We appealed to the public. As we stood upon the streets of Melbourne and played those stirring romantic tunes I often saw the tears start in the eyes of passersby. There's something about

Italian airs in particular which really gets to the heartstrings. The only trouble was that sentiment rarely stretched the pursestrings and whatever we took back to The Violin Factory had to be split five ways when the day was done. Often we'd get back with barely enough to put in the kitty for the night's lodging, and it was not as if Philli ever expected much from us.

The Violin Factory was always there, our haven and our refuge. It was the meeting place for anyone who was really interested in music. Many a night AW Morrison, the American who produced 'Lilac Time', would come along to listen. He was a great collector of violins and respected Philli's judgement. Muriel Starr often came and listened and sang with us, and occasionally singers from the Opera dropped in.

'You've got a future if you stay with us,' Philli told me.

'You could do very well with Mora and me if you'd forget those Wogs and Dagoes,' Dr Richard Rowe said.

Chapter 7

An Evening with the Hangman

Once you've sniffed the Queensland heat and watched that sun rise in the hard, blue sky each morning, the memory is scorched into your very bones for life.

As soon as the cold southerlies blow up from the Antarctic and nip at your fingers and toes, your feet itch to be off again up into the sunshine. It doesn't matter that within a week you're gasping for southern coolness again; your body has tricked your mind into forgetting the discomforts of the heat and nothing seems better than to be grilling like a chop from dawn to dusk.

Two years had blunted the memory of my last trip. I was eager to be on the road again, taking my chance in the country towns, waking up each day in a different place.

'You are such a restless one,' Philli grumbled. 'You did well at the Show this year, you always have plenty of work with us and there is also your friend the Doctor. Why do you always have to be so restless? Think of last time you went when you said you had all that trouble? So much even worse could have happened to you.'

'But I came back with the birds, didn't I? Look how much they've earned for me. If you don't go and look you'll never learn anything different.'

'But you have to travel such a long way in this country to get anywhere at all. So much can go wrong.'

I remembered his words about six weeks later. I'd worked my way up to Sydney and then struck inland over The Great Divide for Bathurst and Orange. In each town I'd stopped a few days, my fiddle playing and the little birds had been well received and I was delighted to have my pockets full for a change, when sickness laid me by the heels outside Dubbo.

I was camped on the outskirts of town on the banks of the Macquarie River, and feeling so sick in the stomach that I wasn't sure if it was best to stop quiet in the shade or shift myself to find a doctor. My guts were grinding and every couple of minutes I was throwing up, except there was nothing left to throw up and that can be the most painful condition of all.

The birds were in their cage on the back seat and Masher lay beside me looking out of the corner of his eyes every so often. No tucker for them either, not a thing to give them for their tea.

'It's a fine pass to come to,' I said to Masher. Talking aloud can have a settling effect on the mind. 'One sick man, one starving dog and a cageful of neglected birds. I'll have to shift myself and find some food.'

So I dragged myself up and washed my face, the sickness not being so bad when I was upright. I went off to the little shop I'd noticed as I drove down to my camp.

'Two pound of dog biscuits, packet of seed. And I'll have a pound of milk arrowroot,' I told the old woman behind the counter.

She said nothing, just looked at me.

'You've got an inflammation in your lower bowel,' she said, and fixed me with a beady eye. Wrinkled as a prune, she stood no higher than my shoulder and was so skinny you'd think a moderate wind would have blown her away, yet she radiated strength and wisdom.

'Are you a clairvoyant?' I asked.

'I don't need to be no mind reader to see what's wrong with you.'

'I'm sick to the stomach all right. Been getting worse since last week.'

'Bin eatin' pork?' I nodded. I often cooked up a pork chop for my tea over the campfire.

'Poison! Good as poison to the system. The graveyards is full of good people who've ruined their digestive systems by feeding themselves pork and shellfish and muck like that.'

'Like it says in the Bible?' I asked her. It began to make sense. 'You get your teaching from the Bible, Missus?'

'Bugger the Bible. I'm a healer.' She puffed up that skinny old chest of hers as if she could put St Peter, St Paul and everyone else in their places any day she wanted.

'Drink this!' She'd flitted off and come back again with a glass of white liquid while I was still standing there wondering about anyone who could be so high hat with the Bible and not be struck by a thunderbolt. Not that I'm a religious man. There's something there, I know that, but I just reckon it's the Spirit of the Unknown. I don't reckon we're meant to know too much here on this earth, but all the same, blasphemy always gives me a nasty feeling down the back of my neck.

'Drink up. Your pain will go soon. Siddown over there. You'll be right.'

And I was right. Five minutes earlier I'd been in such pain I'd hardly known how to put one foot in front of the other.

'Let yer stummick settle down,' she told me, bringing a glass of water to where I was perched on an old packing case by the door.'

'What do I owe you?'

'Nothing needed,' she replied firmly.

'Aw go on, you've done a good job here Missus.' She shook her head.

'Tell you what, then. If I was to read your palm would you give me the secret of that medicine of yours?'

'Read me palm!' she cackled. 'And what'll you tell me? There's a tall dark man who's going to sweep me off me feet? There's a pot of gold buried in the roots of the old gum tree? Go on with you, reading palms is nonsense. Anyhow,' she added, 'the formula isn't mine to give, belongs to someone else.'

'A secret like that's a gift to the whole human race, I reckon. Should be shared.'

'Well you'd best tell 'im about it,' and she nodded her head in the direction of the town.

'Who's he?'

'Chap that knows all about the formula. I'll tell 'im to come and see you.'

That night as I sat by the campfire I sensed someone was outside in the darkness watching me. Sitting beside the glowing logs I was as obvious as a moth on a globe.

'C'mon, c'mon, siddown. Take the weight off yer feet,' I called to the shape that hovered outside the ring of light. 'Siddown mate. No one here 'cept me and the dog.'

Slowly, hesitating all the while, he came into the light and sank on his haunches by the fire. A heavily built man with a shock of hair, he sat there cracking his knuckles, rocking to and fro ever so gently, as though making up his mind to speak.

Masher slunk away with a growl and sat watching, alert and uneasy from the shadows.

His bony fingers cracked again and again as a smile crept across that man's face. A terrible smile, more a rearrangement of the features into something he might have remembered for a smile once, long ago.

'You read the palms?' he asked, very softly. Masher growled again from the darkness.

'None better.' It was a bit of an exaggeration, but Madame de Rossi and Mystic Mora had imparted some of their knowledge to me. The rest you could see for yourself with a bit of commonsense.

'I'm a trifle curious to know about my future, a trifle curious,' his voice tailed off to a whisper ... or was it a hiss?

'None can tell you truer. The palms don't lie. Your future's written in your hand from the day of your birth. Just needs the skill to interpret. It's all there like a book if only you know how to read it. Why, I was telling a young lady in Sydney she was about to move in high places and what do you think I saw in the paper next day?' I paused, this usually started the ball rolling. 'Fell off the top of Farmers she did! Never fails, the palms.'

Even my old stock joke didn't break the ice.

'Read mine,' he thrust his hands towards me.

'Now I'd be very happy to, like I told the old lady. But I've a favour to ask of you in turn.'

'What's that?'

'The formula. I'd like particulars of that wonderful formula. Reckon it's the best medicine I've ever come across. Cured my stomach straight off.'

'The secret's mine.'

'And so's mine,' and I tapped my head with my forefinger and looked at him straight. 'I'll keep my reading right inside of here mate ... and if you think you'll find many dropping off in a place like this with the skill to read the palms, then you're a stupider man than I take you for.'

He considered for a long while, his fingers never ceasing to move and his eyes deep and brooding.

'Tell me what's been,' he thrust trust his right hand at me, 'and I'll be the judge as to whether you've really got the gift.'

That hand! Never in all my life do I want to read a hand like that again. A heart he'd never had, nor a head which stayed true to it's allotted course for one moment. There were things marked down in that hand which sickened me even to think about. He'd been vain, cruel, greedy and weak. I told him straight, there was no good beating about the bush and he took it all, rocking to and fro ever so slightly as though keeping in time to some ceaseless rhythm deep inside.

'If you've seen what's already been so clearly, then you can tell me what's to come. I'll write down the formula for you,' he muttered and gave me his left hand.

Wretched soul. I could only feel pity for a human with a conscience as dark as his. He must have been cursed from the moment of birth.

I looked long and hard at his hand. What could I tell him? The future was not as clear as the past and yet I knew that if I'd seen evil in his past then even greater evil was yet to come.

'You'll be wealthy,' I told him, that was plain as a pikestaff. 'There'll be plenty of money in your pocket. There'll be women too, beautiful women and plenty of them, always there for you to take. Money and women! There! Should be patting yourself on the back, you should.'

I didn't tell him though, that the money was the wages of death and the kisses of the women would be the kisses of sin.

'You're a clever man. Here, give me that bit of paper,' and true to his word he wrote down the formula. I could tell he was well pleased with the result of my reading and quite happy to part up with his secret. But for myself I think I had the best of the bargain.

He slipped off into the darkness as silently as he came, with never a word of thanks. He just handed me the piece of paper and was gone. Masher immediately returned and sat by my feet, shut his eyes and slept the sleep of a wise dog who's made his opinion of a nasty specimen of the human race quite clear.

For me to meet up with that man again was a chance so rare that I reckon it could only happen to a travelling man like myself. Shortly after the war our paths crossed again.

I was showing The Electric Lady at Hobart Regatta and on the next pitch was a strip show. All set up and ready to start when I arrived, and blow me, who should be at the paybox but this bloke.

The Harem, The Dance of the Seven Veils and a few assorted specialities kept those girls busy all the time. There was a Chinese, a black and a blonde. Not a bad class of girl considering, all of them decent types, working hard and not getting much out of it, but him raking the cash in at the box all right.

He looked considerably more prosperous than when I'd read his palm in Dubbo all those years back. Certainly my prediction about the women had come true and I wondered about going over to remind him of the matter, but somehow I couldn't bring myself to approach him.

His eyes were set deep and hooded under his brow. His hands forever moving, his voice compelled the crowd to come and watch those girls. I didn't feel comfortable about him at all, and no one on the ground chatted to him either. Everyone kept clear of him and although the crowd poured in to watch those girls stripping off, no one paused to pass the time of day with the owner.

A startling change came over him the second night of the Regatta. Instead of sitting at the box he was all over the place. His face was livid with excitement, his hands clawing at the air, eyes darting here, there and everywhere, and his voice was completely different. His cries and shouts now rose shrill above the crowd, peaking to a scream of excitement.

'Step Up! Step Up! This way for The Persian Garden.'

'He's going well,' I mentioned to the hot-dog man.

'He'll be off tomorrow.'

'Hasn't been here long.'

'He's done what he came to do.'

'You'd think he'd stop on. He's pulling them in like clock-work.'

'Full to the eyeballs with rum, not surprising really.'

'Why's that?'

'The hanging. Haven't you heard about the hanging in the jail today?'

A man named Thompson was hanged in Hobart Jail that morning. The town had been buzzing that morning, and everyone was really stirred up. Sometimes I think if they brought back public executions people like me would be out of work from the competition. Human nature's very morbid.

All evening that bloke was out front calling them in, his eyes gleaming with the thrill of his morning's work, the rum and the girls. He'd come for the hanging but while on the job made a bit extra with the girlie show.

I'm not saying murderers shouldn't be hanged but who should the hangman be? He would have relished the noose around the neck. He'd have enjoyed the last struggle.

I saw him once again, in Adelaide. He'd got an act in the Adelaide Stadium, a hanging act. It was a really creepy show. He had a helper in a straitjacket and he'd string him up just to give the audience a fright.

'Get back to Melbourne!' a voice came from the crowd. 'Get back to Melbourne! It was you hanged Colin Ross.' The whole stadium was full of shouting and cursing men.

That man made a mint. I wonder if my reading his palm encouraged him to take the path he did? It was a lonely path he'd chosen, a most hated and feared trade.

The only good that man ever did that I know of was to give the world the wonderful formula. As soon as I got into Dubbo I found what I needed at the chemist for making up the draught and I've always had it by me, ever since. So simple a child could make it but more effective than a whole dispensary of medicines.

When I got up near the Clarence River I came upon the strangest sight I've ever witnessed in all my life. I'd camped as usual, outside of town, near the river and away from any larrikins who might be around. I was a bit disappointed when I saw another car drive up quite close to my camp.

I didn't own the place but I'd got there first so I walked over to have a word and saw a sight which set me back on my heels.

The car was just about jam packed with apples. Boxes on the back seat, boxes on the floor, a box on the passenger seat and apples all over the floor. It was a wonder he could use the brake or accelerator.

Sitting in the midst of all these apples was a young man with a bag of apples on his lap and one stuck in his shirt pocket.

'What's the idea? You selling apples?'

'It's me cure.' He took off his shirt and showed himself.

He was a running sore with the weeping eczema.

'I've spent half me life at the doctor's or the hospital but I've finished with them now. This is me last throw. One of them nature doctors has told me that if I travel with a car full of apples

I'll lose me sores in no time. But look at me still!'

He got out of the car, pulling up his trousers and kicking off his shoes. The sight was so terrible I had to turn away from him. The eczema had burst through the skin in hundreds of places and blood ran from some of the festers. His underwear was stuck to his body with dried clots of blood.

He was desperate. His eyes were red and face lined with tension. 'It's the end of me. This apple business hasn't done a thing. I'm finished now. Eight years I've had this weeping eczema. I was a fine figure of a lad – never a day's illness, then out of the blue this struck. No one wants a body like mine around. People think I've got the clap, some ignorant ones even think it's leprosy! It's a curse and I'll never be rid of it. That's why I've come down here.'

He was ready to do away with himself.

'Lost my girl, lost my job, lost everything. I'll finish myself off and be done with it.'

'Wait on,' I told him. 'What about all the medicine they've given you over the years. None of it worked? Think back.'

'Whad'yer mean?'

'Think back if any single mixture did you any good at all.'

He took out a suitcase crammed full of ointment and lotions. Round bottles, square bottles, deep blue liniment bottles and little china unguent jars.

'Useless,' he moaned. 'All useless as the dew on the grass. I've wasted me whole bloody life listening to quacks and healers. I'm finished. These sores will eat into me and I'll be rotten to the bone.'

Poor chap, he was no more than my own age. It was a terrible fate. Something would have to be done, I couldn't just stand there listening to a chap like that talking about doing away with himself.

Suicide is a downright evil, I believe. Killing yourself is a really bad example. Others follow an example, humans being much more inclined to follow a bad one than a good one. That's why animals are so satisfactory, they follow their instincts instead. Instinct is straight and uncomplicated even if it can be very cruel at times, at least it's honest. But humans twist and bend their emotions and torture themselves with things they don't rightly understand, and then when some really sick person has got himself tied up in a miserable state of mind he takes the wicked way out. He kills himself.

Others start to think, 'he did for himself, saved a lot of misery', and before you know what's happening some poor bloke who was only a bit downhearted at that particular time and just needed to be told to look on the positive side, takes the step and tops himself too. And there's no going back.

Never speak of doing away with yourself! To take away your own life is the wickedest thing a person can do. Negative thinking in its worst form. Besides the violence of the act and the upset to everyone around you, you set a pattern. It's like throwing a stone into a pond and seeing the ripples spread. Those ripples affect everything else in the pond, they tip the water lilies and splash the reeds. That one action sets other actions in progress.

'Wait on,' I told him again. 'There's always another chance and you don't want to hold it against those healers. It might be just that the individual ingredients didn't work for you. Get me that bowl out of the back of my car. There's always a last chance.'

I washed my old enamel bowl in the river and dried it very carefully then I took out each bottle of lotion and jar of ointment and tipped them into the bowl, swilling them out and scraping them to the very bottom.

Orange, black, dark brown and lots of pink and white greases and oils swirled about in a mixture of a terribly livid colour. I mixed and I stirred and all the while he watched me listlessly. The smell was a fine mixture of iodine, calamine, alcohol, Friars Balsam and aromatic oils. Then I put in a few drops of the formula for good luck.

'Strip yourself,' I told him, speaking very firmly as though I knew for certain what I was up to. He took off every stitch and laid under one of the willow trees. I plastered him from head to toe, the eczema was even in his hair and ears. I covered every inch of him till he looked like an Egyptian mummy.

'You'll have to stay here all day,' I told him and settled myself down to keep any strangers away. No one came, though. We were in a very lonely spot. The day began to hang a bit heavy so I sat and played the fiddle, let the birds stretch themselves. For food we ate some of his apples.

His state of mind was still very morbid the next day so I

stayed with him and continued the treatment, not trusting him to have the heart to press on. By the time three days was up I'd had my fill of apples and my mind got to fancying all sorts of things like steaks and sausages and jam roll ... but all we had was apples. Apples for breakfast, apples for dinner and apples for tea.

An uplifted heart is the best tonic in the world. If you keep on telling a person they are getting better, nine times out of ten they do. Each morning I scraped off the ointment and looked at his sores, making sure I only said cheerful things about his recovery. I never allowed him to take a good look at himself in case he got disheartened. As soon as I'd examined him I'd cover him up quick with a fresh layer of mixture.

When I wiped off the layer of grease on the final day I was able to tell him quite truthfully that the outbreaks between his toes and behind his knees had gone completely. The others were improving and not one spot of blood oozed from them.

'You'll have to camp here a few days more to let yourself dry off,' I told him and fetched him some provisions from town before I left.

He was well on the road to recovery when he shook my hand for the last time, grinning from ear to ear. Quite beside himself with excitement.

'And to think ... the cure's been here all the time. All those years! It must have been something in one of those lotions which did the trick. Or maybe just a mixture of a couple of things which fixed it.'

But for myself I couldn't help wondering if it wasn't the little dash of my formula that had fixed him up.

Whatever it was, that experience set me thinking. Maybe I had a gift, even if it was only positive thinking. After that I kept my ears and eyes open, whenever I heard of an old cure I made it my business to get the details. These days people are at the doctor's for the slightest problem, they fill themselves up with antibiotics till they wreck their insides. Then there are those who get mixed up with hospitals and seem to welcome the surgeon's knife ... well, once you've been under the knife your natural rhythms are wrecked.

I reckon I learnt a lot from wise old women and clever healers. Certainly enough to keep myself out of the hands of the medical profession.

Once again I headed for home. I was twenty-four now, and many would say a successful man. Never owed a penny in my life and a future ahead of me which was assured as long as my health kept up and the old Model-T did likewise.

When you are on top of the world you get big ideas and my big idea now was marriage. I'd met this lovely girl, Rose she was called, fair haired and pretty as a picture. We'd first made acquaintance at a picnic up at Brisbane. She was a girl from those parts.

She was willing to have me, and did not even mind leaving her folks and coming south to live in Melbourne. I'd never reckoned on being lucky enough to find such a lovely wife. So on this journey home there were two of us in the old Model-T.

By the time I'd got back to Melbourne I reckoned on staying put for while. There was the flat to fix up and married life to get used to. I did not reckon on travelling for a while yet. Dr Rowe was overseas and Mystic Mora was not in the best of health so there wasn't any work in that direction. The Violin Factory was still the meeting place for all the street musicians of the city and going out with the lads on the streets was a bit more relaxed than all the shifting from place to place.

The only trouble was that there's not much to be made when you're part of a band. People are inclined to drop the same amount into the box whether there's one of you on the pavement or three. Still, I liked the company, and loved the sound of us all playing together.

Chapter 8

Dave, the White-Eyed Kaffir, Auntie Lulu and the Dancing Duck

Racing's a mug's game! They can say that again, and I learnt the hard way.

Now that I was having to stay and raise a family, I began to look around for other ways to boost my income. Over the next couple of years I found that supporting them took a lot more than just keeping myself and the birds going and the old Model-T on the road. Foolishly I decided to try my luck with the horses and I very nearly ended up right down the drain. A lesson I've never forgotten.

I chanced to meet a chap called Antonio at Graham's Athletic Club in Collins Street. He was a keen amateur boxer who made his living from riding. He'd just had a good season and was on top of the world, which is an infectious state of mind and soon spread to me.

Easy money's a great lure. I can say that true enough, for I've never been lucky making easy money. All I've ever had I worked for, and worked very hard too. Still, I'd a lot to learn, and with five other fellows I leased a horse called Don Calais and set about racing him in the pony races at the unregistered meetings in Melbourne.

He won five races, straight off. I really thought I was made for life.

'Be careful Owen!' Philli warned me. 'Gambling's no way to live your life, take care.'

I paid no attention. On top of the world I took on a second horse named Golden Gleam, and then a third, Sweet Bobby.

Then I began to lose. Especially with Golden Gleam, nothing seemed to go right with the animal, and it's always been at the back of my mind that there was some funny business going on. I wasn't truly one of the racing crowd; they're a world unto themselves. I didn't know how to go about finding the truth of the matter. I felt I was being conned somewhere along the line.

Then I did a very foolish thing. I borrowed money. That money soon went and I borrowed more to keep up the payments on the first lot, always hoping one of the horses would come good.

Never before in all my life had I been in debt. All I really owned was my fiddle, the birds, Masher, the Model-T and a few bits and pieces of furniture in the flat we rented. Soon I was up to my ears to the tune of several hundred pounds. Those three horses were eating their heads off, spending half their time with the vet and seeing who could be last past the post.

I wanted out. But getting out of such a situation is a darned sight more difficult than getting in. There were the three leases to consider.

Try as I might I was getting very little out on the streets with the Italians. Dr Rowe had come back but had not felt up to the entertainment business any more. With the worry about the horses and the time I spent out busking, I had no time to go making the sort of contacts Mystic Mora used to find for me and the birds in the fashionable charity world.

Being short of cash is nothing when you're on your own, you can always manage. When you've got a wife it's a different matter and now young Ian had arrived too. When you've got responsibility half the joy goes out of life.

Feeling a bit down I was really looking forward to the Melbourne Show that year. I was reckoning on filling my pockets again. People are always generous around showtime. The children tug at their parents' hands and wheedle the pennies out of them and you do very well indeed.

I counted on the Show to put me to rights. Unfortunately I had not reckoned with that sad fact of life that the faster you earn the faster you spend. There were repairs on the old Model-T, then the weather wasn't too good and the crowds did not come around in their usual numbers.

I was nowhere as successful as I'd hoped that year, and to cap it all I had a real dust-up with a couple of sailors who tried to mess around with the birds and got my face bruised. So I didn't look too good either. One slack afternoon I wandered off to have a look-see how the other showmen were managing.

As I passed the boxing booths a medium-sized fellow caught my eye. Not very heavily built, but sturdy and keen looking with fairish hair and eyes that saw right through you.

'Try your luck?' he called, but I shook my head.

'Can't afford to get myself bashed about any more mate. It's the fiddle playing you see, if I damage my hands I can't play the fiddle.'

'Don't kid me,' he laughed. 'You're more a fighter than a fiddler I'd say ... going by your nose.'

'I'll fight when I have to.'

'Yer reckon?'

'Undefeated I've always been. Only use my fists for emergencies so to speak. I'm over there, come and have a look. Over there near Abdullah.'

Abdullah The Indian Fakir was a real draw that year. He brought little chicks out of his sleeves and ping-pong balls from all over his body. Those ping-pong balls popped out from behind his ears, down his nose, under his arms, between his toes. You couldn't keep your eyes on any part of him long enough to see where the next ball was popping out from. Then he did The Rope Trick ... cut his neck in half with the rope, or so it seemed. He was very cunning, a first rate magician.

No! Perhaps not first rate, but let's say very good second rate. First rate magicians are those like Dr Richard Rowe or men like The Great Levante. By the time he retired it was reckoned The Great Levante's wife had been sawn in half more times than any woman living on this earth.

'Abdullah's one of mine,' the man said. 'One of my boys.'

'And who might you be?'

'Name of Meekin ... Dave Meekin.'

Everyone had heard of Dave Meekin. Some said he was a fly one, some said he was a hard man, some said he was the best bloke in the business. Whatever folk said about him one fact was certain, he was not the kind of man you could ignore.

He came over and watched me as I tuned up the fiddle and brought the little birds out onto their perches, but I sensed that most of the time he was watching the crowds' reaction to me, not looking at me himself. When I'd finished with the birds I went on to play 'Just a Song at Twilight' for two old ladies who stood all misty-eyed looking at the birds and thinking of their lost families and lonely twilights. Then I brightened the crowd up a bit with a short rope trick and finished off with the sword swallowing, making the downing of the electric light globe the finale.

'First rate little show you've got there,' he said when everyone had moved off. 'First rate. Mind a suggestion or two?'

'Feel free.'

'Mate of mine, name of Captain MacFarlane, is coming over from Perth. First rate fire eater ... fire eating's a wonderful draw. If you started with a bit of fire you'd have the crowd round in a jiffy.'

Captain MacFarlane put me through the fire eating routine. Cost a fair deal but worth every penny of it. Besides the money I paid him for the knowledge, there was the expense of benzene and cotton wool torches; still it was a good investment. Fire eating's a deal simpler than sword swallowing. The secret's in exhaling rather than inhaling, but beyond that I won't go. There's many a good man making his living from fire eating to this day and I'd be spoiling the act if I let on.

From that time onwards my friendship with Dave Meekin never faltered and it only finished with his death. He was the truest pal a bloke could have. You'd count yourself lucky if you were Dave Meekin's friend.

Dave had a clean cut way with him, coming from being so straightforward ... not false in any way. He loved show business and a good trick or illusion was a delight to him. He was successful too, all on account of his wonderfully logical brain. Never lost track of events, kept strict note of all that went on and worked towards each goal in turn. He acted positively and made events come his way.

Unlike many of the other showmen he did not like his family to be involved in his way of life. He believed they should have something better and kept them separate from the mixed crowd he associated with. Without his family around him like so many of the showmen, he needed someone he could trust and he depended on me right from that first meeting. Soon I started handling his money for him, doing all the banking and a bit of spruiking too when he was busy with the boxing booth.

Besides running the sideshows he was a fine boxer, and at the time I met him was in his prime. He'd stand at the entrance to the booth and take on all comers, none excluded. One night I tried to stop him but he'd have none it. The day before his arm had been broken, his left one too, his guard. The following afternoon a welder from Prahran smashed his nose in. He was a dreadful sight. That evening he was taking the money at the paybox with his damaged left and still fighting in the booth with his right. All comers he took on, never beaten, that night or ever after.

Dave was an intelligent man, he knew boxing would be no good when he was past his prime, and anyhow his wife was dead against it, so he was intent on gathering around him some really good showmen. Together we'd travel, share our fortunes good and bad.

'Get rid of those horses and come along with me,' he said. 'Horses are no good to people like us. You've lost your money, you've learnt a lesson. Only mugs don't learn by their mistakes.' Dave lent me the money to pay off my debts, I finished with the horses and followed him north from Melbourne for the first of many times.

I always came back there in those days, but I wasn't very popular at home. Although I looked after my wife and the two young ones it would not be true to say I was a family man. I always longed to be on the open road or in front of an audience, and there was no way to manage it but to travel.

Our marriage lasted about fourteen years and for many of those I was away from home. I'm not saying I'm proud of that but it was no good trying to alter my nature. I respect women, had many dealings with them at the shows and I don't take them lightly, but neither have I ever wanted to get too mixed up with them. I had a good wife, then Ian and Julie, fine kids, but that side of my life has always been secondary to me. You could see some men mess up their whole lives over women, tie themselves in knots, lie, steal, even murder for them. Not me. With me it's been the shows, the little dancing birds, my dogs and the friends I made.

In the coming years I nearly always travelled with Dave. We went round the circuit regular as clockwork, following the agricultural shows and carnivals. The public think our life is glamorous and exciting. Maybe it appears so, but like any kind of life, if you want success and prosperity then you work for it.

I'd say in a showman's life you work harder than most because apart from presenting your act you have the travelling and the maintenance, the constant concern about the weather and the worry in case things go wrong. You've only got yourself and your own ingenuity to fall back on.

*   *   *

After the Royal Easter Show in Sydney we'd pack up and be off to Bathurst, then on to Orange, Wellington and Dubbo and up to Ipswich for a tour of Queensland. Our northern section would begin with Gympie and did not end till we reached Cairns, and by August we'd be down in Brisbane. After Brisbane we went south again and down to Wagga, then on to Adelaide and Melbourne for the shows in September. Then we'd come back to Kyogle, Lismore and Murwillumbah. After that we'd thank our lucky stars for the four week stop in Southport for the Christmas Carnival. The new show year began with Maitland, Newcastle and Cessnock, and after that it was time to refurbish our acts and prepare for the Royal Easter Show again, maybe making a short trip to Toowoomba for good measure. We were on the road for forty-two weeks of the year.

'Step Up! Step Up! Come and see The Human Vampire. Refused his mother's milk at three days old and cried for a bucket of blood!'

The Human Vampire, The White-Eyed Kaffir, The Pygmies, Half Man Half Woman, The Globe of Death, The Wonder Boy Canadian Glass Blower, The Wild Man of Borneo gnawing away at a shin of beef in his deep pit; this great host of sideshow personalities made their way round the circuit before and after the war. Some making the grade and now comfortably off in their old age, some who disappeared from the scene and live on only in memory.

There were the one-man shows like Pitpot Smith The Strong Man, and Major Wilson The Maori who had an egg-hatching act. Then there were the large-scale operators who ran their enterprises in a businesslike fashion. Some employed up to forty people at any one time and had a dozen or more trucks and trailers on the road.

There was Jimmy Sharman and his Boxing Troupe, Barton's

Follies, and George Sorlie and Sorlie's Follies. George travelled all around the country, set up his huge marquee the night before the show and then entertained each following night. He was a fine singer and an elegant performer. His daughter, Maisie, had The Girl in the Fish Tank. The Girl ate bananas, smoked cigarettes and did all manner of things in that tank. Maisie also had The Headless Woman. The Woman lay in a black velvet draped coffin and a neat arrangement of mirrors cut off her head from view.

'Shocking, boring life for a girl,' I told Maisie. 'Just imagine! Lying there hour after hour while everyone just gawps at you.'

'Makes no difference to her,' Maisie snapped. 'Dead from the neck up anyhow, that kid.'

Arthur Greenhall was another big time operator, starting life earning 2/3d a week delivering for the local chemist and ending up proprietor of The Great South China Troupe and shows like Fun in Hades. The Great South China Troupe were jugglers and acrobats who he'd fetched over himself from Hong Kong when they were on the run from the Communists.

Pedro Labb, like the Italians from The Violin Factory, had come over to this country quite a few years before. When he was about fourteen he used to play the violin on the streets of Melbourne. His speciality was jumping on the trains and playing up and down the corridors. He always wanted to do his own thing. He began to work on the shows with what they called 'joints', that is darts and 'knock em downs'. He married a lady over in New Zealand and they came back here.

His family came out from Italy when the children were very young. There were five brothers and three sisters. They came from a place called Viggiano where they had owned a number of vineyards. The original aim had been to set up a fruit shop but it was Australia's gain that some of them went into the entertainment business. Their family name was Labattaglia. Vincent's real name, then, was Vincent Labattaglia, but he shortened it to Pedro Labb.

I suggested that Pedro took a look at The Swiss Skaters on St Kilda Beach and soon he had that act on the road.

The St Moritz Rink was only twelve feet square, run by an old Swiss, Professor Cortesi, who employed two English girls, Vera and Elsie. The old Swiss had trained them, and years later he retired to run a roller skating rink at Wagga with Elsie, whom he had married. Vera brought some new blood into the act and carried on with it, and eventually it was called The Ice Follies. That skating rink was a roaring success; it even travelled around New Zealand years later.

Professor Cortesi was typical of the old showmen, inventive and always willing to try something different. The rink was a wonder for its time, kept cool with freon gas. During the war the committee connected with the Special Services got them to work on top of the cathedral in Brisbane, to entertain the Americans. The Professor also brought back a shooting range from Paris ... when you shot a bullseye it took your photo. He also brought an organ from Germany, that eventually went to Luna Park. But the ice rink was his pride and joy.

Pedro Labb, Dave Meekin and Les Levante, the great magician, were responsible for establishing the original amusements at the Easter Show. There are others who claim the honour but all who know the history of the showground will back this up.

Those showground people had wonderful close-knit families. Your strength lay in your family. The selling of vacant lots of land in the country marked the beginning of the decline in the travelling show, and films and television were the final nails in the coffin. The public became too sophisticated.

What would they say today to Auntie Lulu and The Dancing Duck? Auntie Lulu Foster travelled with Nell Sharman, the Fat Lady ... Nell ate a whole chicken at a sitting and often took along a twenty-four stone lad with her as her 'son'. He could put away a whole joint of beef, a pound of chips and a three decker cream sponge without having to pause for breath.

Auntie Lulu's Dancing Duck was not to be confused with the Chinaman's Dancing Duck. His duck danced all right, poor bird! That Chinaman hid a candle under a tin plate and it hopped like mad for the audience ... Auntie Lulu's duck was treated like one of the family.

The duck was put on a big box and Auntie Lulu would say 'Bow to the Ladies and Gentlemen!' Ducky would bob down the moment she spoke. No one could see that Auntie Lulu had a bit of string leading to a trapdoor in the box. When the door opened the duck saw a pile of grain underneath and started to reach for it. From where the audience sat they could only see the duck making a bow to them.

Then she'd say, 'What does every nice girl do when she kisses her young man goodnight?' She'd pull another string and a door at the other end of the box fell open and that duck would hop right round and bob its head to reach the grain. Up would come its tail all wiggling with excitement. The audience clapped that duck till their hands were sore, and the old duck got so fat on the food it could scarcely waddle.

Dave was one of the few showmen who travelled overseas, sometimes to Africa, sometimes to Ceylon, and later New Zealand. He ran the boxing booths, Abdullah the Indian Fakir, sold balloons, showed The Five Legged Horse, did buck jumping, and apart from all these he was always on the lookout for novelties. He was the man who brought the first pygmies to this country. Ubangi came before the war, a tiny little woman no higher than my waist, and later on he brought over a whole troupe and they were a show attraction for many years.

We've shared many good times, but even when disaster was staring us in the face I'd choose no one better than Dave to stand beside. He always kept the show going, always came out on top.

The nearest we ever came to hitting rock bottom was up in Rockhampton. We'd been hit by the tail end of a cyclone. This cyclone struck on the night we arrived, and inside half an hour the showground was a wilderness of scattered canvas, fallen branches, flapping banners and drunkenly leaning poles, with cursing showmen running all over the place trying to lash it all down.

Next morning when we checked over the mess we found three tents had been badly ripped and one of the trailers was pinned under a fallen tree. After we'd got a rope around the tree Dave got into the largest truck and began hauling on a rope but as he dragged the trunk across the uneven ground he hit a rock and did his sump.

He never said much when things went against him. He just walked off whistling, with his hands in his pockets and slammed his trailer door shut very loud.

'Reckon sometimes it'd be easier to give the whole bloody shebang away and take a regular job,' was all he said when he could bring himself to talk to me.

We'd just spent a miserable half hour adding up our assets

and our debts. We'd paid the ground rent in advance, nothing owing there, but we were in no state to put on a decent show to get the cash we needed for repairs to the trailer and the truck, not to mention food and petrol to keep us going.

We had twenty-five pounds in the kitty and then Abdullah shot through.

'His sick auntie in Tamworth,' Dave groaned.

'Hasn't she kicked the bucket yet?'

'Not her. Keeps recovering when they've all given up hope. But she's got twenty thousand pounds to leave and he makes sure he's around when she's real poorly. Just so he's not forgotten. Anyhow that's him gone for a week. Did you see my boxing gear? The state of it all! So that's out. We'll never cover ourselves, not even make enough to move on. It's just like I said ... I dream of a regular job sometimes. Like him over there.'

'That baker! You're joking, you'd hate a life like that ... trudging round the streets with that darned great horse for company ... and all ... '

'Wait on, Owen!' he muttered under his breath. 'Ever seen such a horse before?'

That horse must have been twenty hands high. Not what you would call a handsome beast, more striking, and very bony with it.

'Wasted! Wasted he is, pulling a cart around the streets.'

'What do you mean – wasted?'

'We could show him, we could.'

'Aw go on ... haven't we got enough on our plates?'

But there was no stopping Dave. Forgotten was the trickle of oil seeping out from under the truck, the shattered poles, torn tents, battered trailer in its sea of mud, even the absent Abdullah. He offered the baker twenty quid of that last twenty-five and christened the horse on the spot.

'Ajax The Wonder Stallion! The Biggest Horse in the World! What do you think of him, Owen?'

I hadn't the heart to say exactly what I thought. That he was a lot of horse that would need a lot of food. But I'm prepared to admit that Dave had one gift that I didn't and that was vision. He could see possibilities.

Then and there he set to work with ribbons and spangles and a pot of paint and got going on some harness he had lying around in one of the trucks.

The dust rose from that horse's hide like a cloud of grit from an old carpet. Dave combed and oiled his coat until he shone like a new coin. His mane was trimmed, his tail smartened up and his hooves painted shiny, jet black.

Ajax was draped with a golden cloth to hide his bony ribs. Dave fixed sequins to his reins and around his head a silver band stuck with bright red glass buttons which shone like precious stones. On top of that were three great ostrich plumes which gave the illusion of even more height.

'Stir yourself Owen,' he shouted. All I could do was stand and stare at the magnificent beast which was appearing before my eyes. 'Use your nut ... get out your Eastern rig.'

So I blacked my face, put on my Prince Ranji turban and trousers and inside a couple of hours had the banners painted and out in front of the one remaining undamaged tent.

'Come and see Ajax the Biggest Horse in the World! All the way from the Orient. The first time the Sultan of Arabia has allowed one of his prize stallions to visit foreign shores. Step up, Step up! Ajax has carried the Sultan to victory in his campaigns against the wicked Turk! He's taken his Master through the snows of the Himalayas! Come and see The Great Ajax, don't miss the rubies of the Sultan around his head. STEP UP! STEP UP! AND SEE THE FAMOUS CHARGER.'

'Watch it!' whispered Dave. 'I'm off!' The baker who had sold us the horse was at the paydesk.

'Come and see the Wonder Horse,' I called. 'This way sir, the one and only visit of The Wonder Horse, the Biggest Horse in the World.'

That man paid his money with the rest, he stood and stared at Ajax and agreed with everyone around him that it was the biggest horse he'd ever seen. And just think! The silly dingbat had had that horse between the traces of his cart for years. He'd been sitting on a darned fortune.

We made over a hundred pounds with Ajax and got back on the road again. Down at the Royal Easter Show we made four hundred pounds in just a few days showing.

Later Dave improved on the act by importing Little Jimmy from South America. Little Jimmy was only twenty-four inches high at the shoulder. Dave painted his hooves gold and dressed him like a miniature charger. The contrast was stunning, helped along a bit by Dave always setting Ajax on a bit of a mound and digging a slight pit for Little Jimmy.

'Ajax The Wonder Horse and Little Jimmy. The Biggest Horse in The World and The Smallest.'

They were regular money spinners. The best kind of act in many ways. Animals being simple and not given to temperaments, not forever arguing amongst themselves and having sick aunties who needed visiting.

People can be very tricky to work with. Always up or down, rarely to be depended upon. Strong Men, Fat Women, Legless Wonders, Half Men-Half Women ... you can keep the lot! Give me an animal act any day. Treated kindly and looked after well they're far less trouble for a return on your money.

When I went on the road with Dave I bought myself a fine, sound, secondhand tent thirty feet by thirty-five. With the old Model-T pulling nearly as well as she'd always done I was well set up.

By now my act had become a really good one-man show, and with my own tent I could spread myself and do a bit of everything. Fire eating, sword swallowing and besides that I played the fiddle and the harp too. I had the birds of course, and for the first time I was able to exhibit The Electric Lady.

The Electric Lady was an original idea of Dr Richard Rowe and he sold me the gear for a tidy sum. She was a winner, especially at night. The Lady put her foot upon a box of high frequency apparatus designed by the doctor, which I'd helped construct. When the frequency became high enough sparks flew off her fingers and she could light cigarettes from her toes. Besides The Electric Lady I'd also bought a coffin from the doctor and could do Cutting The Lady in Half, depending if I'd got a lady of the right size for the job, which did not always hold ... so that was a more problematical performance, you might say.

Besides this I filled in with a fair deal of magic and illusion I'd picked up over the years. Rope tricks, mind reading, hypnotism and some of the classic acts like Carl Herz' famous flying birdcage act and Ken Rodd's birdcage. Everyone has seen the magician taking the bird out of the cage, putting it in a paper bag, firing a revolver and blowing the bag to pieces. Lo and behold the bird's in the cage again! There were endless variations on that theme. I could keep an audience on their toes for two hours at a stretch.

I was known as Captain Lloyd most times, because I had to keep up with all the Professors and Doctors and suchlike on the showgrounds. When I wore my turban and blacked my face I was Prince Ranji. Prince Ranji did the Cup and Balls and the Indian Rope Trick. I was very successful too as The White Mahatma. The Mahatma had an air of majesty about him, the white tails and little black pointed beard were very distinguished.

But I think I had most fun as The Atomic Healing Wizard who specialised in fortune telling. It kept me hopping, people were always out to trick me, like taking off their wedding rings before they consulted you and asking smart questions to make you look silly. Finally I bought an old slot machine and fitted it up to give forecasts of your lovelife and health and money prospects, but that took a bit of the personal touch away from the Wizard. I only had to add some general background colour then, as they stood and studied the little card the machine threw out. It's amazing how people will take a thing from a machine they won't have a bar of from another human being.

You need to be very strong for that kind of life, you have to be very determined and ready to defend your rights and stand no nonsense. After driving half a day you set up in some backwoods town, like as not with precious few amenities and just a crowd of larrikins hanging about on the off chance of something to pick a fight over.

You pitch the tent, get a bite to eat and start calling them in. First the kiddies, then the older ones. You're kept hard at it till nearly midnight. Never flagging, never looking tired although you'll have done exactly the same thing in front of just the same sort of people a hundred times or more ... and listened to the same mystified whispers.

A smile on your face, a joke on your lips, never move jerkily or look exhausted though your body might be crying out for somewhere to lay it's aching bones. Once you start being slipshod you're finished. You must be as bright and cheerful for the last person as for the first. Never once, however provoked I might have been, did I curse or use any bad language. Who'd let their kids in to a performance like that? Best to keep off foul language in both your private and public lives because if you get into the habit when you aren't in the public eye then one day it'll slip out.

After the last ones had left the ground there would be the birds and the dog to feed, the gear to stow and the tent to strike. In the heat or in the cold, even if the rain was streaming down we'd all have to get down to it and strike our tents, pack up and be off on the road that night getting a bit of mileage towards the next town.

We'd pull off the road finally and I'd spend the night in the old Model-T. I'd fitted a hinge to the passenger seat so it laid back and made a bed. Wherever we stopped I'd be dead to the world until morning.

You needed to be strong for the life or else you needed to belong to a showground family. Nearly everyone else in the business had relatives to back them up. I was alone ... except for Dave.

A solitary showman is a target for everyone. He's so busy looking after his show he can't be watching everyone, so if people feel like getting the better of him it's easy. Besides, there's a lot of jealousy towards an act like mine. No one could compete. I was very versatile and it's a sad fact of life that if people can't get the better of you one way they'll try another. If you're a better draw than the next bloke ... watch out!

Once coming back over the Dividing Range I'd just gone down nearly three thousand feet and was on the flat again when my wheel flew off. Some rotten dingo had loosened the nuts. They'd hoped I'd collect it as I came over the top. If the wheel had spun off there I'd have been finished all right.

On one of the showgrounds I came across a woman with performing doves. She was nicely spoken and very ladylike, and expressed great interest in some of my birds.

'Lovely little budgies Captain Lloyd ... you've got the touch of the master with those little birds.'

She offered to give me a hand, just holding one or two items. Then she left and I went on to the rope trick. The show continued for an hour or so and then I came to my final act which I performed with the birds. I undid the string of the canvas bag where I kept them during a performance but they didn't come hopping out as usual. I shook the bag very gently but still nothing, and then I looked inside.

They were squashed flat. She must have turned away from me and squeezed the life out of those poor little budgies while I was busy with the illusions. She had the heart of a serpent and I in my foolishness did not realise it.

I could have strangled her with my bare hands as I looked at the mutilated bodies of my birds. What good had it done her? There was enough for both of us on the showgrounds. Did she think I was incapable of training another troupe of budgies?

The reasoning behind an evil mind is very hard to follow. Senseless, ignorant and vicious people are best avoided like the plague. If I hadn't been able to look after myself I'd probably have ended up just as tragically as the Pin-Headed Chinaman.

He was a helpless little person, just as innocent as my budgies and just as cruelly treated. The Pin-Headed Chinaman was a tiny man no bigger than a child. His hair was fixed upwards in a pigtail which stood right on top of his head so he really did look pin-headed. He didn't do much, was just a novelty on the showgrounds. Just a sweet natured little person who did no one any harm, and I daresay made a lot of money for those who managed him. He'd been smuggled out of China when he was quite young, but politics were changing in that part of the world and when it came time for him to return no one knew how to get him back without landing themselves in trouble.

He was told he was going home and, poor simple soul that he was, he believed them. When they reached the Timor Sea those he was travelling with tipped him overboard for the sharks.

You have to be very careful who you mix with and make sure you pay your way too. Be beholden to no one, depend on no one's good nature. Every trick I've learnt I've paid for on the nail or learnt fair and square by watching the masters and then nutting it out for myself. I've kept myself free of attachments in the shows, made lots of friends but always known just how far I could go with them ... excepting Dave, of course, who was true through and through.

Dave T. Meekin was born at Atunga Springs outside Tamworth in about 1891. He began working on the land at the age of ten and was self educated. An avid reader with a keen mind, he'd travelled the world since he was sixteen. He was a

Owen playing his home made fiddle. The soloist in the mouth of the horn had the best voice of all the birds.

Owen giving a bottle of beer to a crocodile in Queensland.

The Boy from Buninyong.

"WHAT'S UP, OLD PAL?"—Fondling lions is Dave Meekin's new amusement.   He can have it.
(See article on Page 10.)

Dave Meekin, lion tamer and Owen's close friend.

A poster advertising 'The White Mahatma Show'.

Dave Meekin used to send the pygmies back to Africa for six months of the year, a period he spent travelling the showgrounds. He was superstitious and would not allow them to be photographed before a show.

Betty Broadbent, the Tattoed Lady.

Wee Jimmy, the South American horse that performed with 'Ajax, the Biggest Horse in the World'.

CHINESE WONDERS

CHANG, the Pin Head Chinese.
Weight, 18lbs. Age, 22.
CHONG, age 57, height 28 inches.

A GREENHALGH AND JACKSON ATTRACTION.

Curios of Australia's show days. The 'Pin Head Chinese' was murdered on his return trip to China.

Les Levante, Australia's greatest magician.

AT SHOW GROUND
LI FEN SHAN (From Shanghai)
CHINESE GIANT
World's Tallest Man
NEARLY 9 FEET HIGH.
33 YEARS OLD, AND OVER 30 STONE IN WEIGHT
Says the Giant (through an interpreter): "I will give
£50 to any man who can reach taller than myself."
Presented by Afrikander Dave T. Meekin.
Whitmarks Ltd., Pr.nt, 102 Sussex Street, Sydney.

MYSTIC MORA PRESENTS ORIENTAL MYSTERIES
PAINTINGS IN COLORED SANDS

Lloyd's of London
PRESENTS
The ATOMIC
HEALING WIZARD

Owen Lloyd with The Electric Lady.

The Busker of the Year entertaining crowds in a Sydney pub.

Owen and friends at Dave and Florence Meekin's grave.
Ubangi is at the front.

"BEST OF THE BUSKERS"
1979 ABC CONTEST
KATE FITZPATRICK
BOBBY LIMB, JEFF STONE
AND MYSELF & THE BIRDS

Owen after winning the ABC 'Best of the Buskers' contest in 1979. He is pictured here with Kate Fitzpatrick, Jeff Stone and Bobby Limb.

fighter and was mentioned in Les Darcy's book on famous Australian fighters.

I'd like to think I modelled myself on Dave, but I reckon that would be very difficult because Dave had that wonderful gift in life which eludes so many of us. He found love.

Love's always around in varying forms, from lust to just sheer duty, but not many of us find the real article. He married his childhood sweetheart, Florence Brown, whose family were hotel keepers in Tamworth. He loved her all his life and kept her and their daughter Beryl clear of all worry and trouble making sure their lives were separate from the showgrounds and that they had all they needed.

'It's no place for a respectable woman,' he always said.

Beryl grew up a very talented girl. Later she became one of the Tivoli artists and she put her success down to the fact that her mum and dad gave her such a wonderful home. Dave was a strict teetotaller. He never swore; the worst I'd ever heard him say of another man was, 'Get that ape out of my sight.' He never allowed cards in the house, and the only time he found a pack in Beryl's room he tore them to pieces in front of her. I was one of the very few people he kept close around him. He trusted me to do his banking and manage his affairs when he went overseas.

Loving his wife as he did Dave listened to her advice and the advice of a sensible woman is often what makes a man in the end. First of all she took a dislike to boxing. Said she wasn't going to be married to a punch drunk bloke. Many a man would object to his wife interfering, but when you love someone you listen to them and she had real sense. What was the point of him standing up night after night against drunken sailors, hefty country boys and some of the half-baked giants that promoters seemed to be able to pull out of the hat night after night at the booths. Brute strength leaves us all in time, it's brains that counts ... that's what Florence said.

So Dave began organising others, and that was how he got into the lion taming business. He brought out Captain Lindo to the first show of all held in Lismore. The lions turned on Captain Lindo and nearly ripped him to pieces ... what was Dave to do? The Captain was in hospital and would be for many months and the show had to go on. That was when Dave first went into the cage with the lions.

Florence hated this, and couldn't see the sense of her beloved Dave risking his neck each night with the lions. 'I've got a wife and a fat baby to keep,' he'd say. 'Well there must be safer ways of doing it,' she'd reply.

I've never known how Dave managed it but he kept that part of his life away from Florence. Didn't tell her too much about the lions, occupied himself with his other shows – he just ran the lions too on the quiet.

All went well till Florence took young Beryl to the St James Theatre in Sydney to see the pantomime 'Jack and The Beanstalk' with Afrikander and His Lions. It was a matinee; she and her mother were sitting in the stalls dressed in their best when it was announced 'We have great pleasure introducing Afrikander and His Lions'.

The lions came loping on followed by Dave in a white satin suit. Florence fainted on the spot.

'Poor lady,' the woman in the next seat said as they tried to revive her.

'It's not as dangerous as it looks dear,' another one said. 'There's always someone out the back with a gun ... just in case.'

'No there ain't!' retorted Beryl. 'That's my Dad ... he doesn't even own a gun.'

Florence had to be carried out from her seat and that was the end of Dave's lion taming days.

He wasn't game to upset Florence by continuing with the lions so he concentrated on bringing different showmen to Australia from overseas. Eventually he gave the lions away altogether after being badly clawed at the Melbourne Tivoli. He gave two of them, Maudie and Elsie, to the zoo, and two others to Sole's Circus.

A great succession of acts passed through his hands. There was The Chinese Giant, then Half Fish Half Girl, different pygmies over the years, the Kadamas with their horses. He cared for their welfare too, he didn't just use them and shrug them off. Little Jimmy ended his days on Dave's brother's farm, Beryl has still got his golden shoes.

The Meekins were great-hearted people, and it all sprang from that wonderful feeling those two had for each other. Florence died very young, only forty-two, and it broke Dave's heart. They were lovers till the day she died and he never looked at another woman. He became a solitary man, lived at the Canberra Hotel at Kings Cross, went out each day for his meals and down to the showground. He was polite to everyone, charitable to anyone down on their luck, but he kept to himself.

Chapter 9

Two Girls in my Fishbowl

The only illusion I never paid for was The Girl in The Fishbowl. Being blessed with a good mind when it came to working things out scientifically, I invented this one myself.

Dave reckoned we needed something a bit more artistic to amuse the crowds. We'd got some clever acts between us but none that you'd call particularly artistic. The Electric Lady was more stunning than alluring, and the Lady Cut in Half more horrifying than pretty.

I fixed up a little booth with strong lights focused at the correct angle and we'd get a girl to strip and go through the old routine, working under very bright lights. Then by a series of prisms and lenses the rays of light were converged into the Fishbowl which was outside the booth, giving the public the lovely sight of this little lady dancing in the Bowl. No more than five inches high ... they were spellbound.

This act became another money spinner, far better than the run-of-the-mill strip shows since it had artifice to recommend it and everyone was mystified about how the illusion was created. I never lacked for strippers either. I never had any trouble getting girls to strip for me ... whatever their mothers might have thought about it.

At least I didn't have any difficulty until I got to Balcleuth and for some reason I wasn't so fortunate. Try as I might, no one was willing to do a bit of stripping. The Girl in The Fishbowl was a major attraction; I'd had the banners out since early morning and people don't like being disappointed.

I scratched my head and puzzled over it half the afternoon until two young lads caught my eye, over near the Fairy Floss. Nice looking lads, not too big and bony and yet with good legs on them. Young lads are always a bit short of money at showtime so I decided to approach them.

'Want to earn a few bob?'

'You bet we do sir,' one of them said. 'What do you want sir?' the other one asked.

'I need a bit of help tonight, nothing difficult or dirty, would you like to come back here and have a look at the set-up?'

And so that night I had Two Girls in The Fishbowl. I fitted them with long blonde wigs and little two-piece bathing dresses and painted their faces. They were a riot, my Girls in The Fishbowl. No one guessed except a pair of queers who came by.

'Bless me, I swear they've got balls under those costumes,' one cried to the other. Which goes to show they can recognise their own kind quick enough when there's a bit of hanky panky around.

We were doing very nicely and I thought no more about it till I heard there was a woman in the crowd looking for two boys. Her son and his mate hadn't come back from the show and it was getting late.

'Over here Madam,' I called, and showed her The Fishbowl.

Those two boys were swinging around to 'Tea for Two' and slipping their bathing tops on and off every couple of minutes. They were having a really good time.

She wouldn't believe me at first but the more she watched the more she became convinced. I was lucky really, she could have turned nasty, instead she started laughing fit to bust. Laughed and laughed and then went off and brought all her friends along. Being matron at the local hospital she insisted anyone who could walk should come down and see The Girls in the Fishbowl. I made a small fortune that night.

*   *   *

Fate stepped in and put a stop to all that kind of life in 1939. I'd been kept with my nose so close to the grindstone that I'd not noticed there was a huge old world out there getting into a muddle. Happily spinning around the circuit, Queensland, New South Wales, Victoria, South Australia, it had never occurred to me that my life could be altered.

For the first few months of the war I performed around the schools back down in Melbourne, raising money for comforts for the troops, but very soon I was drafted to the Beaufort

Division down at Fishermen's Bend. My engineering knowledge had always been a great help in life. Keeping the Model-T on the road, fixing up trucks and trailers, sorting out the mechanics of The Girl in The Fishbowl, constructing my fiddles. I'd never forgotten my early training at Mackay's and I soon settled back into work as a fitter.

At least my fingers, my arms and my body did but how desperate I was to be away! Now I knew what it meant to be a bird in a cage. For years I'd set off each morning with a new sky greeting me and each night slept in full view of the stars, taken my chance where to eat and who to talk to.

The confinement of the factory was terrible. I'd stare at the high brick walls and focus my will on them, longing with all my soul to see them topple down and show me the trees and bushes and grass beyond. But of course such foolish thoughts are only negative thinking and deserved the disappointment they brought.

'You're getting thin,' Philli told me one day when I called in on him. There were no more gatherings at The Violin Factory, he was a solitary old man, still repairing fiddles, still playing to himself in the twilight but nearly always alone.

'It's the caged-in feeling, Philli. Sometimes I feel I'll bust if I have to stand amongst those chaps for another minute. They all seem happy enough, the money's good, but I feel my whole body is shrinking from their company and the dreadful boredom.'

'There's many would think you're lucky. What about those who are being shot to pieces, what about those in concentration camps, eh?'

'Mebbe, but I'd rather take my chance than stick in a place like the factory. I miss the shows so much. I miss it all.'

'Then you'll be going to the Capitol next week?'

'Why should I go to the Capitol?'

'For the auditions.'

'What auditions?'

'The Great Levante is running auditions for entertainers. People will be picked to go and entertain the troops.'

Les Levante had come back from England at the start of the war. He was one of the greatest showmen Australia ever produced. He had been made Prince Rat of the Grand Order of

Water Rats in Britain, one of the great honours of British showbusiness. He would have been King Rat except he felt he should be back in his own country in wartime.

Glad and Les Levante went to England in 1933. He was an international illusionist. Together with Glad he travelled around the world for fifty years. Glad was a beautiful woman, one of the first women in Australia to play the accordion. She worked with her husband all the time. Their daughter Esme went to school in Belgium. She was a very clever girl, who spoke and sang in English, German and French. She performed in cabarets all over Europe.

Les Levante soon took me on. Within a month I was with the Special Services entertaining troops and earning twenty-five pounds a week.

The Special Services came into their own when the Yanks entered the war. I joined the Stars and Stripes Revue and went up to Brisbane. There were a lot of big camps around Brisbane and a sea of faces would confront us performers on the racecourse when we put on a show. Yanks everywhere ... some tall and gangling, some fat and bespectacled; they sent over a real assortment of chaps. They never looked as healthy as our lads, too much soft living compared with us. You couldn't help feeling sorry for them though, they looked so out of place, so aimless in a strange country like ours.

I'd left old Masher with Dad back in Melbourne. He'd never been in the act and as Dad had taken a fancy to the dog I decided he'd be best at home. Now I took in Little Ruby, The Writing Dog, a clever little animal who was a first class performer never needing to be told twice. A dog is a fine sight for soldiers, it reminds them of their homes and their families and their own hearth. A dog can bring tears to a man's eyes. Little Ruby pulled her cart, sat up and begged and wrote on a blackboard with the aid of a magnet. I had to slip a metal cover on her paw, but no one was any the wiser.

Illusion is a wonderful art, a cool head and a steady hand are the only tools you need ... and above all a confident smile. Doesn't often go wrong, but when it does it's the smile that helps you most.

With Little Ruby, the birds, the fiddle and the fire eating I had a very pleasing act. At first I'd had the sword swallowing but that didn't last for long. I was called before the commanding officer after my first show.

'That dog of yours, she's mighty fine,' he began, getting a bit conversational. 'The boys sure appreciated your show last night, but I'll have to ask you leave out the sword swallowing in future.'

'Why's that sir?'

'Well, they'll shortly be facing the Japs, and I consider that seeing the sword go down could have an unpleasant effect upon my boys' minds. The less they think of swords going down into their bellies the better.'

So I had to forget about sword swallowing for the duration. Before the end of the war the Special Services ran down their efforts and I was offered the position of manager of the little circus at Taronga Park Zoo in Sydney. There was Tommy, the Timor pony, the last Timor pony to come from Java before the Japs got there – they are very highly bred, and the Dutch would never allow a female to be exported for that reason. With Patch, the Shetland, I had the two of them waltzing, jumping hurdles with monkeys for jockeys and putting on a fine little all-round act.

I learnt a lot about animal training while I was at Taronga Park. All along the line it's patience that counts – if they think you are going to ill treat them you'll get nothing from any animal. One day the young lion I had in the show ripped my hand open, he tore it right to the bone. There was no reason for that, I'd never ill treated the animal. Sure enough, when I asked around I found the truth. One of my helpers had been seen teasing the cub, slapping him across the face with a glove. Once you ill treat any animal they never forget and can bear a grudge against the whole human race, which is why if you are to be a successful trainer you are best always handling the animals yourself, never allowing another person near.

The war left me feeling very restless. Wars are great explosions of the cosmos, completely negative happenings, and it takes time for the clouds of chaos to settle and things to return to normal again.

When you get that restless feeling you don't always take the most sensible course and that's how I came to try a spell in vaudeville. 'The Old Woman In the Shoe' was one of those shows really meant for children but which everyone goes to because in the towns where we were showing there wasn't much else to do anyhow.

I was The Bad Baron and I was really so evil and bad that the kids fairly shrieked at me for all my devilry. They'd yell and holler at the Poor Old Woman to beware. When I came to turn her out of the Shoe I thought they'd be up on the stage after me. I was a really bad, Bad Baron. So much so that when I left the theatre after the show the kids would be waiting for me at the stage door and they'd boo me down the street. That made me feel really good ... I knew I'd done a good job and I'd hurry off, looking over my shoulder and scowling and shaking my fist at them, just to keep it up.

I did a fair supporting act with the fiddle and the birds, also some fire eating and sword swallowing, but I was dressed in my Prince Ranji outfit then and no one guessed it was the Bad Baron entertaining.

If those kids had only known! The really bad one was the Little Old Woman. Straight as a corkscrew he was and as AC/DC as they come. I caught him one day backstage making up to some of the little children who'd come round. I laid him out flat. Just laid into him with a couple of good blows and that was the last time I saw him interfering with children.

The whole atmosphere of the theatre can set a person off on the wrong track, I reckon. Some people go quite crazy about the life, get themselves in love with the smell of greasepaint and lose all sense of reality. When I used to smell the mustiness and catch the faint whiff of mice and stale beer in the dressing rooms I'd long for the open air of the streets and the showgrounds again.

'Comin' round to my place after the Show?' The Magician suggested one night. 'It's me birthday.'

'Going to wear your birthday suit?' I laughed, not thinking properly, which I should have done because he gave me a really knowing look.

Everyone from the cast was there. The Little Old Woman, the Broker's Men, Fancy Pants the Komic Kat, Bo-Peep and Little Boy Blue, all of them.

'Have a lamington luvvie,' Buttons urged the Little Old Woman.

'Not me ... I'm sweet enough as I am,' and he batted his

eyelids very coyly and wiped his sticky fingers on his bra. He made a lovely woman, the only thing that gave him away was his Adam's Apple. You can always tell the boys from the girls by their Adam's Apples – a useful tip if you want a quick check.

'Ooh! Look who's here – our Feathered Friend! Sorry duckie, we're clean out of birdseed – here have a chip!'

I felt about as welcome as a pork chop in a synagogue, and was just about to give a smart back answer when in came the Magician.

He was wearing a skimpy pair of pink drawers and something lacy round his chest. There were three long, pink ostrich feathers on a sequined band about his head, and in his hand a huge fan of the same pink feathers. 'By a Sleepy Lagoon' was being played very loudly on the gramophone and that Magician swayed and shimmied all round the room in front of us.

It was enough to make a cat laugh! I couldn't help it, I laughed till the tears ran down my face. No one took a blind bit of notice of me, they were quite enthralled with the sight of their mate doing the light fantastic.

They were a sight to behold. The Little Old Woman in his bra and satin dirndl skirt, Buttons in gold lame with a chocolate eclair half stuffed in his mouth and the Broker's Men spilling the Red Nell all over their satin harem pants because they couldn't take their eyes off the Magician. Bent as a dog's hind leg.

I couldn't stop laughing. Tears ran down my face and my stomach ached so I thought I'd bust. It was then I decided I'd quit the vaudeville stage. I wasn't fitted for such a complicated life.

Chapter 10

Across the Indian Ocean

If anyone had told me when I was a young lad standing in the icy wind on the racecourse watching for those pigeons that one day I'd rest my fiddle against the trunk of a coconut palm and watch the baboons run helter skelter among the rocks while the maribou storks circled overhead, I'd have told them straight they were heading for the cuckoo tin.

'Ever thought of Africa?' Dave asked one day. 'You've no idea what it's like over there. They'd never have seen an act like yours. You'd make a mint. Besides, there's business to be done.'

Dave had his heart set on bringing back some more pygmies to Australia and he wanted to see what else there was to offer.

'I'll be going over soon with the buck jumping, you get yourself a berth and follow on, and we'll meet up over there. The Trust'll have plenty to keep us busy.'

'The Trust?'

'South African Amusement Trust. They run most of the shows in that part of the world, and send them round the rest of Africa too.'

The more I thought about Dave's words the more I considered the idea. I'm not a great one for books, but if I'd ever chanced to read about the place it certainly sounded exciting.

As far as I could tell life was shortly going to fall back into the same old pre-1940 pattern. Coming back to that after the war was very pleasant and reassuring, but there are many years later on in a man's life when all he wants is security, and I felt I hadn't reached that time yet. I couldn't see myself spending year upon year doing the same acts before the same people ... because the faces in the crowd were just about the same, just a little bit older and new kids always filling the seats.

When people remembered me from before the war they came up and shook hands and sighed over the good old days, but I'd wince inside as though waiting for the snap of a trap which would keep me in the same situation for the rest of my life. I could become an institution, like baked mutton with pumpkin and potatoes ... and I'd end up being just about as exciting too. The more I thought over Dave's words, the more I wanted to follow him and have a look for myself.

*   *   *

As the boat approaches the coast, the scent of Africa reaches out to you. A mixture of vegetation, spice and the very essence of life, distilled from seething black bodies who have battled and schemed and loved and lost for centuries, in a cauldron of strife over the fires of tribal beliefs so foreign to anything I'd know before that I could only ever be a spectator.

The moment I stepped ashore in Durban I entered a different world from back home. And what was more I found a new sense ... the sense of smell. Of course I'd always been able to smell things, anyone can, but up to now the sense of smell had been just another tool to see me through life. Was there enough vinegar on the chips? Exactly how old were those chops? Was it time to clear out the animals' cages? The sense of smell was now a blessing and a curse, but whichever way you looked at the question it certainly elevated every experience to a level of excitement I'd not known before.

Australia is an ancient land too, but she's old in a dreamy, lackadaisical fashion. The Aborigines have lived for thousands of years in a waste of desert and rock, wandering over the land, believing in their Dreamtime, making a living in the sparse bush and the lonely places.

Africa is a flourishing garden compared to Australia's dusty paddock. The bougainvillea which in Australia is merely a beautiful climber, in Africa is a wild exultant predator which clambers to the tops of trees and nods to the jacaranda over the white walled gardens. The bottle brushes which survive thriftily in the sparse soil of Australia go mad in Africa, and shake their long red bristles in defiance at the baking sun; and the moon which shines upon the pale trunks of Australian gums, in Africa silvers the tips of the palm trees and coats the streets, bazaars and houses in a white mantle of mystery. I was enchanted and amazed, and all the while a little nervous.

Finding a place to stop first of all wasn't as easy as I'd thought. I'd brought all the gear with me and that was a great heap to cart around. My fiddle, the necessary for The Electric Lady, the swords, a trunk of clothes, my magic box and some extra gear Dave wanted for the buck jumping.

You can't just stop anywhere in a place like Africa like you can back home. They don't seem so used to the varied class of customer who uses the kind of hotels and lodging houses around our country. The whites were very snobbish by comparison and anything else would have been out of the question.

On the way over I'd met up with Auntie Lulu's nephew, Alfie Foster. Alfie ran a flea circus and we decided we'd try our luck together. The first sight wasn't too good, crammed with all our baggage into a backstreet hotel where the company wasn't what we'd been used to and the food was so terrible it got my guts crawling. Next day Alfie remembered the address of a widow he'd been told about.

Mrs Lipton was her name and she'd been in show business in Australia years ago but had left to marry a jeweller who took her to Cardiff to live. After a few years he'd shot through and she'd left Wales to join her married sister in Durban, making a living engraving and setting stones.

We reckoned she'd be a bit more broad minded, having been in the business herself, but she'd come up in the world since then. When she saw me and my mound of luggage she looked as if she didn't want to remember her old days on the showgrounds one little bit. We decided we'd best not mention the fleas so we just told her we were mates and hoped her food wasn't as poisonous as the last night's.

'You'll not be staying long?' she said as she eyed my baggage.

'Not on your life,' I told her. 'Mate of mine has a string of engagements lined up for me, and Alfie here's booked up to Christmas. We just need somewhere to stow the gear and stop while we fix up a few particulars.'

Alfie's fleas were a really hard cross to bear. I've never liked the creatures myself and found it a bit difficult to consider insects as part of a way of life. He kept them on a bit of white rabbit skin secured upside down on his wrist so they could have a good feed and were easy to catch when he wanted them. Either they got bored with the taste of his blood or else they were restless after the long sea journey, but whatever the reason they started to wander, and what with the bellyache and the scratching I soon began to wish I'd not picked up with him.

'Can't think what's bothering little Skipper,' Mrs Lipton kept complaining after we'd been there a couple of nights. Skipper was a highland terrier she'd named after Mr Lipton on account of his wandering habits. 'He seems to have picked up something; I've never seen the dog scratch like that before.'

'You'd best be off,' I told Alfie. 'Once she gets wind of that vermin of yours we'll have lost our lodgings. If you go now I can keep the room on and we'll have somewhere to stow the gear. But if you stop that Skipper'll scratch himself into eczema and we'll be without lodgings when she cottons on.'

Alfie was a cheerful bloke, took it all in good heart and besides that he was sick and tired of cornering that Skipper and searching for his stock in trade back again. Skipper was black and woolly and not the most convenient hunting ground for fleas.

Alfie took himself off to Johannesburg and very soon I had a letter from him. Very depressed and not making much at all, he reckoned Africa was nothing like the goldmine we'd been told to expect.

I almost felt as sorry for him as I did for myself because none of the contacts I'd made turned out to be much chop. Dave came up to collect his gear but he couldn't offer anything from the Trust, we'd struck a bad patch and my money wasn't holding out too well either.

Poor Alfie, he deserved better. You need a lot of patience with the fleas and he was a first class showman in his line. He had a magnifying glass and a pair of tweezers and a tiny hook was fixed under each flea. Alfie would pick the flea out of the rabbit skin and attach the hook to a little cart or a miniature cannon and off would go the flea, hopping like mad and pulling the contraption along. He was a clever man with his fingers, he deserved a bit of success after coming all that way.

As soon as Alfie was out of the way I settled in quite nicely with Mrs Lipton, and even though I felt I ought to have done better, I did finally find a few bookings in Durban.

'It's a bit more cosy now we're on our own,' she told me a few days after he'd gone. 'Two's company but three's none I always say.'

The red light showed for me. I wasn't going to get myself entangled but on the other hand I needed the lodgings so I didn't have to get too distant neither. Each evening after the servant had brought in our supper we'd sit near the open window and Mrs Lipton would explain to me how different Africa was from Australia and how you needed to meet someone to put you right on a lot of things when dealing with the blacks ... not to mention the whites and the coffee coloureds too.

'You could have a wonderful life here, Owen,' she told me. 'Me, I've wasted my life serving others, and me, once the best fortune teller in the business. But there's no need for you to go to waste, fine upstanding figure of a man like you.'

Oh Lord, I thought, the same old trouble with fortune tellers. They always want to help a bloke along who's doing quite nicely on his own.

'My trouble was marrying outside of the business ... birds of a feather should stick together they say. Arthur seemed such a nice class of man but I'd never have married him and left Australia if I'd known the kind of life on offer. Imagine me, Madame Laura, fortune teller to the cream of Melbourne, spending half my life in a shop in Cardiff. Not that I've anything against the Welsh,' she added hastily on account of me having told her about my old dad and Lloyd George and the rest. 'But it's a grey, dull sort of a place, nothing like home, or Durban for that matter. The sun hardly shines at all in Wales and they have a special sort of rain, extra penetrating, which soaks right through you. Chills you to the bone ... and it always rains on Sunday too. Sometimes I think it's a penance on the Welsh being so religious and narrow minded.'

'Couldn't call me narrow minded,' I told her, feeling a bit offended. Then I wished I'd kept my mouth shut because the next minute she was sitting right beside me.

'Not a bit of it, Owen. You're a lovely man. But I'm warning you, you've got to be careful who you team up with in this world, don't make the kind of mistake I made. Never marry a Flaherty, I say.'

A Flaherty is someone who isn't in show business and so cannot understand its ways. I could see Mrs Lipton considered events should take their natural course so I was very glad when I had a letter from Alfie telling me he was fixed up. He wouldn't be needing our lodgings again and so I could be free to travel around.

Dear Owen, Times is changing and Lady Luck's looking over my shoulder again. When are you coming to Joburg? Yours truly never had nothing worth calling a break and I was desperit. Even sold my spare suit when I hit on a wonderful idea. Advertisements the ticket mark my words I went along to the newspaper office with the fleas and I asked to speak to someone in the know. This reporter asked me what I was doing there and I told him Id come along to thank all the good people of Joburg who had been so good to me and for him to let them know in his paper that there fleas were the biggest and the cleverest in the whole world, certainly cleverer than Aussie fleas.

Travelled the five continents I have I told him caught fleas of of the camels in the desert and of one of King of Englands shooting dogs and even a flea of a tiger that was sick in the zoo. But never and I said that three times over had I ever found such A1 kinds of the breed as I found in Joburg. Thyre a credit to you and Id like the good people of this wonderful warm hearted country to know the truth about themselves. Considering Id not got a feather to fly with by then and could not get back to you and Mrs Lipton except if I walked which I never fancy in a strange country I reckon I made a good story. Next day it was in The Star 'The Biggest and the Best in the World. Top of the Flea League' and I've never looked back. Busy from morning to night so you can keep Mrs Lipton and that there Skipper for yourself.

Yours in Friendship. Alfie.

I didn't need to worry either for events were soon working out very nicely for me and the future brightened. I began to work for the Trust on the showgrounds. The shows weren't exactly the same as ours in Australia. For instance, I ran into a bit of trouble trying to find an Electric Lady. I ended up with a chap called Fransicso ... or Fransisca as he was known professionally. He put on a very good show in his hula skirt and satin bra but he landed me in endless trouble outside of the show because our customers were always coming round asking him out.

He was very attractive, with high cheekbones and the longest finger nails I've ever seen, and he'd waltz off with his escort to the 'bio' (what they call the movies over there) or else to a dance. But when they delivered him back at our place and thought matters might progress there was always a terrible ruckus and many nights I had to turn out and help Fransisca give them a belting.

'Can't you turn an offer down? What do you have to go out with them in the first place for?' I'd grumble, still half asleep.

'Can't help it if I turn 'em on can I?' he'd giggle. He thought it was all a good laugh.

The South Africans would have held up their hands in horror at our white Fat Lady or Auntie Lulu and The Dancing Duck. Their shows were confined to exhibiting blacks, and for a collection of strange creatures I'd never seen their equal in all my born days.

We had one chap, a Cape Coloured, who had three legs, eighteen toes and a second set of sexual organs.

'Off with it man,' the Boer farmers would shout, and this chap would take off his cloth and show the farmers' wives his second set of what-have-yous. What a sight he was! The public never tired of looking at him and wondering about him, poor devil. I suppose today most people like that would be shut up inside somewhere since birth, but in those days they made a good living from their deformities. We had a Tall Man, eight foot six inches high, and several Fat Women ... so fat they'd have made our Fat Lady back in Sydney look like a weight watcher, they could manage two chickens each at a meal.

The most famous attraction of all were the Black Spots. They were shown by a man called Elmer Matthews. They'd been found in the countryside herding the sheep. There must be small sheep over there because an Australian sheep would have walked right over the top of them. One of them was only eighteen inches high, and the other was twenty-three inches. They were like perfect little dolls, and the public used to pick them up like babies and marvel at them. They were perfect, tiny people, totally in proportion.

Dave wanted me to bring the Black Spots back when I told him about them, but the authorities knew when they were on to a good thing, and try as I did I could not arrange for them to leave the country.

Dave's real aim had been to bring the pygmies to Australia.

We managed to get a whole troupe back to Sydney. We could combine them in an act with little Ubangi and have a really fine show. Our Ubangi was a lovely singer and dancer, and now there would be Shonna, Jimmy and Solomon to assist her. Years later these three pygmy men returned to Africa, but I wonder if it was a wise thing to do? For humans like them to return to their country was like trying to return a tamed, wild bird to nature again. The flock scent the presence of Man upon the creature. Civilisation has its own odour, and it would be torn from wing to wing.

Poor Shonna was murdered soon after he returned, stabbed fifteen times and even then he was alive, so they finished him off by putting his head under a bus. Whatever happened to the other two we'll never know, but Ubangi refused to return with them. She stayed on all her life in Australia, and was always a first rate attraction at the shows ... she never lacked for anything, and her fingers were covered by great diamond rings.

At the time they left Africa they were young and lithe and a joy to watch as they danced and entertained the crowd. Our life must have been a marvel to people like that, since Africa was a teeming mass of humanity all scratching for a living. Anything that lifted an ordinary person above the common lot was an improvement. The cruelty and poverty were entirely foreign to me. It was not just the thoughtlessness of the whites. They regarded the blacks as lesser humans who needed keeping in their place, but the worst part was the sheer brutality the Africans practised to their own kind.

Ubangi was a gentle little woman, and although born a pygmy and having lived all her life amongst her own people, she was glad to leave them. She felt their ways were brutal and without kindness.

If a wedding was to take place amongst the pygmies, she told me, the little bride was placed in a kind of corset and the older women of the tribe examined her to see if she was a virgin. If she wasn't, they would force her to tell who her lover was and they would both be cast into a pit of fire.

She said that such a life was not for her and even if the others returned to their native country she would never follow them and she didn't. She lived till 1976 in Surfers on an annuity Dave had made available for her, and his daughter Beryl kept an eye on the old lady. There weren't many as true hearted as the Meekins in show business.

I couldn't have stood to spend my life in a country where they were so cruel, but at the same time the beauty and the abundance hypnotised me and I felt I was swimming in a sea of unguessed pleasures and pain. The black people were so kind to us wherever we went, and so faithful too, yet they could be incredibly brutal.

The whites acted as if they were above everyone, and really what else could they do? If they sat upon their verandahs sipping their gin and tonics while half a mile a way some native was cutting the living flesh off a bullock rather than waste the effort of killing it first ... had they much choice in the matter? That was the way of that particular corner of the world, it was best to keep your distance and uphold your own customs and keep to them very firmly.

Of course travelling showmen like myself were a novelty, and perhaps we were an embarrassment to the whites. We weren't up to their way of life, our business caused us to associate with all sorts. We couldn't be treated like the natives because we were sunny white like Sunlight Soap, the same as them, but on the other hand we made our living in a way they'd never have dreamt of doing. No, it was a funny kind of life for people like us.

There's so much trouble there these days but how could such different cultures really mix? The blacks should be left to themselves and their own devices I say, because it's their way and they understand each other. They accept the spiritual side of life in preference to the material, but whites have held up material gains as an end in themselves and the blacks are confused by that.

It is easy for someone like me, coming free and easy from our country, to criticise the ways of others, but for real ignorance you could not beat some of our forefathers. The Aborigines have suffered with us in the past. At least the blacks in Africa weren't wiped out like a lot of ours were. Now we choose to forget about that and act as if we have solved all our problems and the rest of the world should listen to us. We solved our problems, all right, when we let the first wild bunch of British do their work, when they poisoned the food of the Aborigines, when they hunted them for dog's meat and castrated the males and spayed the women.

I once came across a place in Tasmania where they had wiped out the whole population of blacks, herded them to the cliff edge in droves and chained the poor unfortunate devils to stakes at the bottom while the ones left above dug the graves. When the tide came in and had done its work they had to fetch up their mates' bodies and take their own places while the next lot were digging their graves in turn.

When people speak about animals being dumb brutes, I can't help but think that humans are just such brutes, but unfortunately not dumb. If we were dumb we couldn't spread our ideas and carry on with our evil ways. Humans are such cunning beasts, even to the extent of making an animal do our work for us. The only murder I've ever witnessed was committed by a man but executed by an animal. Some would say it's an impossibility, but I saw that happen in one of the circuses I worked with once.

We had an elephant trainer with a string of four fine animals; Mario, Jumbo, Fakir and Solly. He was a first class man and his animals loved him, followed his commands and caused no trouble. It was an unfortunate fact that this chap had a most flashy wife, and she wasn't inclined to keep herself to herself either. Helped at the paydesk and generally made herself of use and available to everyone. The type of woman who causes trouble. She took it into her head that she preferred her husband's young assistant to him, and she made a dead set at him and of course he wasn't backward in coming forward, you might say. In the end he'd have done anything to get her and between them they planned to get rid of her husband.

The lover helped each night with the elephants and knew their ways, knew the words of command and understood how to control them. Elephants are intelligent creatures, and no one need use cruelty on them. When you want them to kneel you tap them behind the ear with your hook and the animal kneels for you. One day the trainer was sick and couldn't go on, and this was the couples' chance.

The assistant went into the ring that night and when it came time to make the elephants kneel, he dragged at Mario's ear and the hook tore into him. The elephant had never had this before and obeyed in fear.

The next night the real trainer took over again, but when he raised the hook to the elephant's ear the animal knocked him over and knelt on him. It killed him outright. Mario was shot of course. Everyone was horrified, thought he'd gone rogue or some such rubbish. But I knew how it had been worked, I'd seen it all. There was nothing that could be done about it though, it was a perfect murder.

From the Amusement Trust I joined Pagel's Circus, the largest in Africa, and I travelled with them as their Ringmaster. I'd never held a position like that before but didn't find it difficult. Circuses aren't as rough and ready as they can be over here. First of all the blacks, whites and coloureds are all firmly separated, and to make sure nothing goes wrong there's always a man patrolling with his whip. Cruel long whips they use, made from the skin of a rhino's penis, they told me.

Everyone sits up high and the man walks around below to see that people keep to their places. One night a black woman up aloft was laughing fit to bust at the clowns, and forgetting herself she piddled right on top of the man with the whip. Beside himself with rage he lashed it upwards and caught her right on her bare bottom through the slats. I've never seen anyone disappear into the dark so quick. She made the audience laugh more than the clowns did.

However mixed my feelings were about Africa, I decided to stay a while, though the money wasn't as good as it might have been. The circus went up to Kenya after a bit, so I decided to stay with it and see a new country.

Kenya hadn't got the strictness about it that South Africa had. It was more natural, I'd say. Going from South Africa to Kenya was like changing from Kraft Processed Cheese onto Gorgonzola ... you'd found the real thing, as far as Africa was concerned anyhow.

The blacks were very faithful, and if you treated them kindly they'd do anything for you. I must say the shifting and carrying was lot easier than it would have been back home. None of us had to do much heavy work, only worry that we had enough money for the animals, feed and transport.

The towns weren't much different from South Africa really, though everything was on a smaller scale. The first difference I found was the horde of beggars on the streets. Never in my life had I seen such malformed creatures, men with no fingers, no toes, and sometimes they were not much more than a torso sitting on the pavement whispering for alms. Then there were children without an arm or a leg and women who were little more than heaps of rags and a pair of eyes peering at you. Leprosy, rickets, and all manner of diseases had brought them to this, and if nature hadn't helped them along the path to beggary, then it was said that sometimes babies were mutilated to produce a twisted body that would earn a good living on the streets.

Compared with the towns, the villages were wholesome places. They were just collections of huts, not proper villages, more like family groupings. A man would buy a girl from her father for the price of a few goats or cows and then she'd come to live in a little thatched hut near his. He'd visit her when he wanted, but always returned to sleep in his own hut. When he was a bit wealthier he'd take another wife and then another. Each wife had to thatch her own hut and when the time came they all got together and thatched his.

The women were beasts of burden to the men. You could see them toiling home each night from their shambas, as they called the little smallholdings, laden with maize and reeds and bananas, or bowed under great bundles of wood almost as high as themselves. They plodded along like wooden haystacks, the children struggling along behind with great tins of water. The men would be sitting around the huts exchanging gossip and waiting for the women to get home and cook their evening meal.

Feeling a bit light hearted one day I asked one of the girls if she would marry me, and she took it for the genuine thing.

'How many cows does your father want?' I laughed not thinking anyone would believe such nonsense.

She came back inside the hour saying that rather than cows, since he was a rich and powerful man already and had a good sized herd, he'd settle for two of the ponies in the circus and he'd be along to speak to me in the morning. I made sure we were on our way that night. I didn't fancy the idea of any disappointed, powerful father descending on us out of the banana groves with all her uncles and cousins and nephews, all wielding those fearsome pangas ... just to press the point, so to speak.

I had to get used to a different type of audience, and I soon realised that if the colours were not the same as back home, then neither were the attitudes to what they were looking at.

I was not regarded just as an entertainer; to the ignorant portion of the audience I was a magician. I was a real-life magician who could perform miracles far better than their witch doctors and perform them to order as well. No sitting around reading signs in the entrails of a chicken or coaxing some god to send them rain. Each evening on the dot I could produce birds from empty cages, swallow swords and eat fire. I was an instant witch doctor you might say.

At first I found the silence which greeted my act rather worrying until I realised that they were struck dumb with amazement and often quite petrified with fear in case the magic should escape from the circus ring and chase them into the darkness.

The Electric Lady was almost too much for them and I could hear that deep growl of fear which is like the breaking of waves against rocks, concealing depths of ignorance which cannot be comprehended and should not truly be exploited. It's a funny thing but I've never felt I deceived people before. I'd just entertained them, but in Africa I did feel that I could be called a fraud. They believed so wholeheartedly, they watched every gesture and marvelled so innocently that sometimes I questioned my own conscience whether I was doing right performing in front of such simple people.

When The Electric Lady stood on her box she was surrounded by a sea of black faces and staring eyes, when I lit cigarettes from her fingers and tapers off her toes they sighed with apprehension lest she should spring up and shrivel them to cinders with her touch. For she must be able to do so, her touch was fire, wasn't it?

I decided to add a small refinement to the act. She held a harmless snake in her hands and as it reared up its head the forked tongue spat fire in all directions. I tried that only once in public. When the snake began spitting there was pandemonium. People came tumbling down from the upper tiers onto the lower in wild panic trying to run away into the night. The poor wretches underneath protected themselves as best they could and dragged themselves under the seats, and soon the tent was a mass of flailing arms and legs.

Never again! That part of the act obviously touched something so vivid in their imaginations that it was best not tampered with. Besides having to consider the ignorance of the audience I found some of the performers were equally set in their ideas and would not always listen to reason. Even when it came close to losing their lives they did not really take kindly to the advice of others.

We had lions in that circus that were a great attraction, even though there were real lions around the place which I daresay everyone had seen in their lifetime. Lions are peculiar animals, you have to be very careful training them and they respond absolutely to the tone of the voice. If you want them to sit quietly you speak gently, if you want them to get up and move about you shout, and they perform their tricks best if spoken to sharply.

When the lions joined the circus I was surprised to find they had a lady tamer, which was an unusual combination as it had certain drawbacks. She'd not been with the lions very long, having taken them over from her uncle, but she was doing well, though she thought she knew everything about the life which is a very foolish attitude when you're new to the business.

I didn't relish mentioning the subject which was uppermost in my mind but I did happen to know a fair bit about lions and as I was ringmaster, I felt I had a real duty to make sure she understood the facts of the matter.

'You do know, don't you,' I asked, feeling very awkward as I said it, 'that if a lion smells blood he goes quite mad ... you just can't have blood near a lion.'

She looked quite amazed and then agreed as though I'd told her something even a child should know.

'Ladies can have difficulties with lions,' I said very pointedly.

And the silly woman still looked blank. Then comprehension dawned and she bit her lip hard, very annoyed. I could understand that, but then it was my duty to point it out.

'I can tell you, man, that I've had no trouble yet and I won't have any,' she said.

'But you could one day. It just needs a bit of bad luck, and if those lions catch the scent nothing can save you.'

But she was that stubborn nothing would have moved her, so I said no more. What could I do? Couldn't take the act out of the circus and, as she said, she'd had no trouble up to that time.

I'm not a man who enjoys saying 'I told you so'. The world is too full of people who could always 'have told you so', but didn't at the obvious time for various very good reasons. I can truly say I wish I'd never been in a position even to think that about the poor lady lion tamer, but she brought it on herself.

She was very annoyed at me mentioning a subject that no decent man would bring up before a lady. She ignored me as much as she could, and nothing happened. She had her technique in the ring well worked out and the lions rarely got too near. She never put her head in their mouths or anything like that. But one day she decided to walk one of the animals around the showground for a bit of publicity – and that was her downfall.

She was menstruating. When the lion caught the scent he turned upon her and knocked her down and that was very nearly the end of the woman.

I was with the ponies when I heard the shemozzle and even as I raced out my blood was cold in my veins. She was screaming in the most dreadful terror. The lion had leapt at her and as she lay on the ground he was worrying her shoulders.

What with the screeching and the running to and fro all around she might have been dead inside a minute, but luckily one of the chaps who'd followed me had a long rake with him, and while he kept on distracting the beast by hitting its back I flew off to the lions' truck and found the stave she used for controlling the animals.

There was silence when I got back, I was sure the lion must have nipped her jugular for there was blood all over the place. The lion was crouching beside her, his yellow eyes watching the rake as the man held it aloft, all the while his tail twitching with rage just like a cat that's been disturbed when it was finishing off a mouse.

I rushed straight in with the stave, pushed the animal back against one of the trucks shouting all the while, until the other chap grabbed its chain and we were safe again.

She was two months in hospital, and apart from the scratches and tears up one side she had suffered such a shock that her insides were all upset and not working properly. Such a fright can be the ruin of your life. It takes the spirit out of a person, but she pulled through in the end. She didn't come back to the circus though, she left me with the lions after that which all added to the work and worry, but no one else would consider taking them on.

*   *   *

When I'd finished my tour with the circus I landed back with Mrs Lipton in Durban. It was a foolish decision because she had her eyes on me. I could tell that, but lodgings were difficult to come by and at least I could stow my gear at her place.

'You don't stay long in one place do you?' she said when I'd had a few days there repairing The Electric Lady and getting everything shipshape for the road. 'Do you have to go off so soon?'

'While I'm here I might as well have a stickybeak,' I said, and that was true. I'd heard about places where no showman had ever been. There was a challenge in moving on and looking for fresh audiences.

'But you said you were thinking of Zanzibar? Now that won't be near as nice as Durban,' she wheedled. 'It's really foreign in those parts, you'd need to be careful 'mongst all them Arabs.'

Truth to tell I thought I'd be safer among the Arabs than with her.

'How about I give you that little room next to mine on a long lease, special terms till Christmas?'

But I wasn't wanting any of her 'special terms'. I'd made up my mind to be off. I was in no hurry to get back to Australia so I followed up the subject again very tactfully, told her I'd only be away for a short while and she agreed then that I could stow my gear, and she'd keep the home fires burning, in a manner of speaking.

Not many places live up to your expectations, but if anyone told me they wanted to travel back in time to the days of the Arabian Nights, then I'd advise them to make the journey to Zanzibar.

A wonderful aromatic scent of cloves filled the air and caught at the nostrils as soon as the ship neared the island. Several miles out you catch the first whiff, and then the smell

114

grows stronger and stronger until it seems that all your previous days have been lived in a dull, odourless world. Light, spicy, all-pervading, the winds blow the breath of the clove far out to sea and bathe every nook and cranny of the island in its fragrance. Zanzibar practically lives off its clove harvest.

I had not taken all my gear, just the fiddle and the swords and of course the packs of cards, so I could move easily without too much trouble. Immediately I found lodgings in a respectable looking lodging house and settled myself in. My room was on the ground floor but the windows were barred and there was a heavy iron lock on the door so I felt safe.

I needed to feel safe because there was an air of mystery and intrigue – not to mention downright wickedness – which made me a trifle uneasy. I was on really foreign ground now, and for one of the very few times in my life I wished I'd had a travelling companion. Even Alfie and his fleas would have been a comfort.

A fat, cheerful Arab named Suliman ran the house and he took it upon himself to make certain I knew my way around the town all right. He had so many uncles and cousins and nephews that I never needed to venture out on my own and for once I was glad of the company.

It would not have been difficult to lose yourself in those winding streets. One led off from the other and unless you pinpointed your position by a certain mosque or a distinctive house or something like that you could wander around in circles. The houses were tall and forbidding, but at the same time the beauty of them fascinated me so that I walked along the streets forever gazing up at the carved wooden eaves, the decorated verandahs, and above all, the magnificent doors. The frames and lintels were a riot of carved leaves and fruit, while each panel of the door would be neatly lined by regular patterns enclosing yet another wonderful design.

Veiled women and men with fezes on their heads hurried about the streets and coffee sellers poured out cupfuls from huge cone-shaped brass pots on the pavement. And the smells! Mixtures of peppery spices, oils and tantalising nutty odours streamed out from behind the wooden shutters and tickled my nose. To look at those strange crowds and think that in some part of their everyday life they would sit around and gossip and plan just as we used to sit around our Sunday tea-table while

Mother poured the tea and Granny told her about the latest scandal in Buninyong, gave me a comfortable feeling. Even if we all looked so different, our lives would be basically the same. People are the same the world over, but it would take a lifetime to understand their different habits and beliefs. If only I had nine lives like a cat how quickly they would rush by! Here I was, in my early middle age, only just beginning to see that the world was different over the other side of the Indian Ocean.

Africa was completely different from Australia, and apart from the obvious contrast of the countryside I puzzled over what the difference might be. I decided in the end it was the number of people about the place. Flocks of humans were everywhere, they filled the many floors of the tall houses all around, peered through the fretted verandahs from second, third and even fourth storeys, and in the evenings overflowed on to the streets like starlings in the trees at dusk. So different from home where humans were sparsely scattered in the towns and properties outside the cities, and even the cities were thinly populated places by comparison.

Men, women and children were everywhere, dozing in corners, bargaining at stalls and filling the bazaars with a huge volume of chatter. So many people indeed that you began to discount them. Like the starlings they were almost a plague on the land and you understood why they were so little regarded. When I looked at the Sultan's palace I could almost comprehend why he had caused live slaves to be built into the walls during its construction. So many people, so many subjects. Did it matter that a few died to preserve him from the evil spirits lurking outside the walls?

Slaves were still being sold in the market place – they looked perfectly happy. After all, they would be going to a life known and understood for generations, and someone would now have to feed them and keep their bodies alive, which was better than beggary on the streets.

Even I felt I was beginning to understand what made them tick though I didn't want to get too closely acquainted with them. Women sat at the doorways of some of the houses beckoning me inside – but what waited for me at the other end of those dark corridors? Not me, I stayed out in the sunlight among the crowds.

Old Suliman was very interested in my act. He gathered around a mass of people each night and they would stand and gaze in wonder as the sword disappeared into my belly and the cards came from nowhere. No one gave very much but on the other hand there were so many of them that the little each one gave soon added up. Best of all they loved to listen to the fiddle. I could have played for hours each night and they would have sat there asking for one more tune until daybreak if I'd agreed. I played tune after tune to that audience sitting under the stars, while the breezes sifted through the palm leaves with a gentle rattle.

'That is a wonderful instrument,' Suliman told me. 'Never in my life have I seen a violin with a horn at the end. A most musical instrument.'

He was offended when I refused to sell the fiddle. I believe he considered it good manners for a guest to offer to do business if the merchandise was openly admired. But where would I have been without my old fiddle?

I needed that fiddle to earn my spending money and see me back to Sydney. Added to that, I was very proud of the instrument. Suliman was right, my fiddle was like no one else's and I'd recently improved it too. I'd fixed a little ivory head to the top of the neck. She looked very exotic now with the grinning ivory face up the top and the big horn down the bottom.

I would not sell that fiddle, despite their repeated attempts to buy. My fiddle had been my constant companion for nearly twenty years. But I should have thought more carefully. I was benumbed by the seething life around me and I wasn't thinking positively. I guessed they'd quite happily slit my throat for that instrument but I thought they'd come at me in a fight and I'm never worried about who comes on top in any fight I'm in. I was thinking with my head and not my heart. I was disregarding the powerful feelings of people who have set their hearts on attaining an object, and I paid for my foolishness.

Towards the end of my stay in Zanzibar I was invited by one of Suliman's friends to perform at the house of a rich merchant. A magnificent man, he stood nearly seven feet high and his beard flowed down to his waist. I was taken to his house and welcomed by the master, surrounded by his male relatives and servants and slaves who crowded the corridors and anterooms of the house.

First of all I was given a meal. A slave brought a calabash of warm water and then dried my hands with a linen cloth, then little brass and china bowls were laid out filled with a great variety of food. Rice with tiny nuts, mutton cooked in various ways and tiny dishes of spicy mixtures like chutneys and pickles. Then came thick black coffee in the smallest cups imaginable, and as my host and his friend sat back I brought out the fiddle and began to play for them.

Even to my ears the sounds were not right for the house. To listen to The Londonderry Air in a room where carpets lined the walls and not a foot tapped nor a body swayed, pinpointed my feeling of isolation. I should have guessed they could see other fingers than mine moving up and down with the bow. I should have realised they wanted that fiddle to play their own tunes and melodies.

'Will you sell the fiddle?' I was asked. Again I refused and at the finish of the evening made my way back to Suliman's in the company of one of his cousins.

After locking the door and for extra safety putting a chair up under the door handle, I shut the window and got myself ready for bed. The fiddle was on the table in the middle of the room where I could be certain to know if anything was up.

I was perfectly safe, I'd taken every precaution. Soon I was asleep but it was a troubled sleep. Somewhere at the back of my mind an old moon-washed landscape was waiting for me. The gums were stirring in the night air, and their branches reaching out to welcome me back home.

I'd stayed away too long, I was uneasy. I could smell the scent of the eucalypt and the air was full of orange blossoms. But was it eucalypt and orange blossom? I opened my eyes and immediately closed them for they stung. Peering through half opened slits and seized with a fit of coughing I realised my room was full of smoke. I leapt from my bed. By the light of the moon I could see a drift of smoke coming under the door. I rushed to open it.

Then I stood stock still and listened. Voices could be heard outside. Not voices raised in fear, but conniving, mumbling sort of voices. The smell was not of burning wood – it had a strange sickening odour like a herbal oil.

Someone had lit that fire on purpose. They were trying to smoke me out and perhaps they hoped to suffocate me with whatever it was. Instead of opening the door I crept over and threw the window open ... after all there were bars across it, so it should be quite safe.

Immediately a long pole was thrust into the room with a hook on the end. Without one false move it hooked around my fiddle strings and dangled the instrument high over my head. I leapt up to reach it and heard the hiss of a laugh from the darkness outside, and there was my precious fiddle swinging away towards the top of the window where there were no bars.

I shouted with rage. I jumped onto a chair and grabbed the pole. Oh what pain shot through me! The beasts had embedded razor blades down the whole length of the pole so that they bit straight through my flesh and I was lucky not to lose a finger.

Pole fishing! That's what I found they called that particular act of thievery. Very popular in Africa. I had to stand there, blood pouring from my wounds and watch that fiddle be pulled through the bars above my head.

In my fury I made for the locked door. With my hand on the bolt I paused. Who waited beyond, how many were there? They had what they wanted. I was now a useless encumbrance. So I sat on the edge of my bed and tied up my hand as best I could. Obviously the time had come to go back to Australia. The dream had showed me the way. I'd lingered too long and I might never get back if I stayed to argue the point about the robbery.

First thing in the morning I left the house of Suliman and that day left the island for good. I went back to the relative safety of Mrs Lipton and Skipper, where the perils were more of a domestic kind.

Chapter 11

New Zealand

'Pity I ever suggested Africa to you if it's left you so restless,' Dave complained.

'Not really restless – just got that feeling I'd like to see a bit more of the world before I settle down.'

'Settle down! You settle down! You must be joking.'

'There'll come a time when my travelling days are over. Might as well see a bit of the world before I'm too old. Reckoning on Europe ... d'you think I'd do any good in those nightclubs they have over there?'

'Europe? What do you want to go all that way for? Right off the beaten track.'

'Back of beyond, you reckon?'

'Back of beyond. No, I'd say try nearer home. How about New Zealand?'

'I dunno.'

'Or the States.'

'Not on your life. All Mafia and cops over there. I've heard what the States are like.'

'Can't see why you don't take a trip to New Zealand, then. No Mafia there, very respectable folk from the sound of it. Bordering on the dull I reckon, but perhaps you could liven them up a bit. Couple of tunes on the old fiddle and the budgies hopping everywhere and you'd have a riot on your hands.'

I didn't take too much notice of Dave – he resented me wanting to be off again, which was understandable. We'd been first-rate pals and he trusted and relied on me. He regarded the whole show scene as a business venture. For me there was still the thrill of sitting in front of an audience, holding their attention all on my own. New audiences are exciting, keep you on your toes. I didn't want to get stuck in a rut for a while yet.

The upshot was that when the century was in its fifties and me likewise I sailed off to see what New Zealand had to offer. Dad said he'd mind the birds and the dog and I set about gathering my gear together.

I crossed over with Vincent Labb – or Pedro Labb, as he was now known. Pedro, like me, had gone ahead in the business and added to his acts. He took The Skating Rink, The Octopus and The Laughing Clowns, as well as his usual sideshows over with him.

I was loaded up to the eyebrows. I had The Electric Lady, The Girl in The Fishbowl, Cutting The Lady in Half, Mind Reading and Fortune Telling by The Atomic Healing Wizard, and a new one called Jasper The Invisible Ghost. Besides these shows there was the fiddle, sword swallowing and fire eating. I reckoned I had an act to suit all tastes.

There was no time at all to look around once we arrived. Showtime never stops, summer or winter. If you do get a few days to yourself then you have to spend it working over the gear, mending and repairing. We were all in the same boat, hard at it as soon as we arrived, never having much behind us either. You could be flat broke one morning after you'd paid the ground rent and got set up, then by the evening you might have a hundred pounds in your pocket. But if you fell foul of the weather or there was some rival attraction like a football match, a swanky wedding or a big funeral, then you'd be back to square one.

First off I bought myself a decent van then got a new lot of birds and a dog to train. I called her Ruby after the other little dog. I joined up with Buddy Williams, the Australian Cowboy, and La Tosca ... she had no arms and did everything with her feet, which was a real novelty. She'd make a phone call, even changed the baby's nappies, just using her feet. Then I fixed up with a stripper I'd met called Lola, to come along when needed as The Electric Lady. She was a most beautiful girl with deep mauve eyes, and she'd fix the audience with that gaze of hers and they'd be in a trance. Her only problem was she couldn't resist the men and I had nearly as much trouble over her as I had with Fransisca in Africa. In fact, within a few days of landing life appeared to have slipped back into the same old routine ... but of course it was the same old routine in a completely different country and that made all the difference.

Hard work occupied me so completely that I did not begin to take real notice of the country till I'd been there a month or so. Unlike Africa, which bombards you with sensations and even reaches out to you as you approach over the water with the strong scent of spice, New Zealand waits for you to take notice of her, almost hides herself, you might say.

The country is a beautiful, unawakened, fairytale land that slowly unfolds its mysteries and in the end completely captures you. Africa fascinated and enticed me to stay longer, but finally my sense of outrage at the cruelty turned me against the place.

New Zealand, on the other hand, hinted at its beauties, then twisted my heartstrings and finally bewitched me with the stories of its past. Fact and fable are entwined in a lore which is part and parcel of the Maori way of life. The Maoris have taken what they want from Christianity and intermingled it with their own legends wherever this suited them and they've come up with a mixture of fairytale, fact and doctrine which explains all to their satisfaction, forgives what should be forgiven, and punishes what should be punished.

I couldn't have stayed in Africa beyond a year without becoming as unfeeling as the others around me. The harshness of everyone's view of each other would have sickened me in the end. Savagery was such an accepted way of life amongst the Africans, that I wondered how they could hope to live peacefully. On the other hand, the Maoris are fine people with a strong sense of pride. Savage in the past, very cruel, but clever with it and possessed of a fine sense of humour.

They didn't chop off the arms of their children and send them begging in the streets, they didn't sacrifice five hundred slaves if the chief died, they didn't do wicked things for the sake of cruelty. In my opinion they were honourable people, people you can stand beside and be proud to know.

I was so busy on the showgrounds that I didn't have the opportunity to miss my old friends back home, but I always liked to make new ones too and appreciated the company of educated men. That's how I happened to be sitting in my tent with The Great Braemar on the Christchurch Showground one day.

The Great Braemar had been studying at Dunedin University, where he became involved in a fight, gave one of the professors a hiding and was sent down. He was an aggressive, impatient man, but I've never met such a clever person in all my born days.

He was a hypnotist and in that he far outclassed me. He could hypnotise a whole roomful of people and have them doing everything under the sun, completely under his control. And the company he kept! Parliamentarians, ministers, businessmen, all sorts ... he knew everybody who was anybody, and people gathered around him like bees around a honeypot. He was a man of great charm and personality despite his bad temper.

We'd been sitting having a chat when he got up to take leave. He must have risen awkwardly because he went as white as a sheet and grabbed one of the poles for support.

'What's up, mate?'

'M'cursed back,' he gasped.

'Get's you like this often?'

He nodded, speechless with pain.

'Here you take my arm. You've got to lie down. Do just what I say. Come on, over here,' and meek as a kitten he let me lead him over to the Coffin.

'Wait on ... I'll put something down to make it soft for you.'

Finally I laid him on top of the Coffin and ran my fingers along his spine. Ever since I was a kid I've been able to rub away aches and pains, my mother often asked me to rub her shoulders. She used to laugh and say I had magic in my fingers.

I'll say this for The Great Braemar, aggressive or not, he knew a thing or two about human nature. From the moment I laid hands on him he gave himself over to me. He'd worked so much with the power of the mind that he understood when it was necessary to let your defences down and trust another person's will.

'Easy does it, easy does it,' I murmured to him, and my fingers explored those vertebrae one by one. 'That's right, relax, just give yourself over to me completely, body and mind.' He didn't answer, he was so far within my power I could feel his body and spirit acquiescing.

I worked up and down his spine with gentle pressure. Not a groan came from him; he lay there passive and unresisting. Time, patience and confidence, wonderful medicine for the damaged body.

'Captain Lloyd, you're wasting your time in a place like this!' He told me afterwards as he sat and watched me brewing some tea in the old billy. 'Why, with your power of the mind ... which is quite considerable really ... and the skill of your hands, you should be a healer.'

'Sounds like the last thing in the world for me,' I told him. 'Healers are religious people, and I can't lay claim to that.' Ever since my early days I'd kept clear of religion, I'd seen too many people come to the wrong conclusions with their minds clouded in that direction.

'Nonsense! You're a fool! Religion can work for you or against you, some healers work from the basis of religion, some work from sheer faith in the strength of the healer himself. Now that would be like you. There's persuasion in your tongue and cunning in your fingers, you're a healer! Healing is an art, I tell you. If you have the ability for it then it's your duty to use your gift to that end.'

I hesitated. I was not anxious to embark on a new life and there was so much I wanted to know about this new country, a different tenor of life to become accustomed to, new ideas and habits.

New Zealand is a slow place, life unfolds about you instead of confronting you as it does back home. Hesitate as I did, events moved to force me in the direction I had to follow. I was confronted with a situation which I could not pass over or ignore.

I had crossed over to the North Island and was travelling up from Wellington hoping to reach Gisborne in time for the Agricultural Show, when I was waved down by a Maori woman at the roadside. She had a little girl with her and because I was travelling towards her destination I told her she could hop in the back with the child. I should have looked at her closer, but my mind was filled with plans and thoughts as to what I should be doing up in the North Island.

The road was bumpy and the day hot and oppressive, and we hadn't travelled more than a couple of dozen miles when I heard a groan from the back of the van. Not bothering to look round I shouted to them, 'You right back there?' There was no reply.

That was funny, I thought. I slowed down and looked over my shoulder. The woman was stretched out on the floor of the van and the little girl was crouching over her.

'Mum says her time's come,' the little girl told me simply.

'Her time?'

'We'll have the baby soon,' she explained.

I stopped. What a pickle I'd got myself in. 'This is a fine time to tell me a thing like that! What are you doing here then? Cadging lifts off people when something like this is about to happen?'

'Not for a month ... ' the woman gasped.

'We'd been with auntie, she's sick, we'd only been there for a few days. She was better and we were going home. Mum felt her pain starting and said we must hurry. Get home quick!'

'You might have warned me.' I was more worried than annoyed, but Nature can play some funny tricks and I suppose the poor woman just never thought, if she had another four weeks to go.

'You'd not have taken me,' whispered the woman.

'I'd have found the nearest hospital though, missus. I'd have found a doctor at least. I'd have found someone. But what can I do out here? I can't go on driving with you like this in the back. We're miles from nowhere.'

We were on the Desert Road, a barren stretch of countryside. The earth was black and gritty, dull green manuka scrub covered the ground and the air smelled of sulphur from the distant craters of Ruahpehu and Ngarahoe. There's no more desolate stretch of road. Evening was approaching, the distant cone of Ngarahoe fast disappearing into the twilight and Ruahpehu silhouetted against the sky.

'What can we do?' the woman asked.

I didn't like the 'we' very much, but the situation was inescapable. You can't tell a baby to stop being born, ask it to wait, tell it to go away until you've driven on and found a doctor.

'How do you expect me to know about childbirth?' I asked them, but the little girl had the light of faith in her eyes ... grown ups in her world would never fail. Her mother groaned and shifted on the floor of the van.

'All right! But how do we manage without water, without anything to keep her clean?' The girl shrugged her shoulders, the woman groaned again. They were no help at all. Obviously I was the one who had to have the ideas.

I laid out my mattress on the floor and covered it with a blanket, and between us we rolled her over on to it. She lay down, closed her eyes and clasped her daughter's tiny hand for comfort.

'You've had children before my dear,' I whispered. 'Tell me how to go about it.'

She just rolled her head from side to side and snatched at my hand as a spasm of pain caught her. She gripped me tight, but even in her agony I noticed that she did not hold the child's hand as feverishly as she held mine. She was a good, understanding mother. She would spare her little daughter as much as she could.

About the only useful thing I did know about childbirth was that everything follows a rhythm. Pains begin at long intervals then speed up until the mother is permanently convulsed as the birth approaches. I took out my watch and counted the minutes between the spasms. Immediately a smile touched the woman's face and the little girl patted her mother's hand. The sight of me crouching beside them, watch in hand, obviously gave them confidence. But how I wished I could have washed my hands, done something to make myself clean. Fortunately I had several bottles of my formula and with nothing else to hand I used it to swab myself.

First of all the pains were every seven minutes but the intervals between rapidly diminished. The tempo of her moans and heavings increased and as I concentrated on her needs I had no time to feel nervous. All the while I held her hand and talked to her, because it was useless to feel ill-used, put upon and forced into this difficult situation.

In between the periods of pain that racked her she listened and I talked and talked. Told her about the wonderful boy she would bear, the joy of her husband and the rejoicing of her relatives. I made her feel the pains of birth were just a necessary prelude to a wonderful fulfilment. A small price to pay for such a marvellous gift that would shortly be given her.

That was all very well of course, but there is a practical side to these matters which cannot be ignored. I shrank from the thought of the blood and the strife of the actual birth but there was no way I could avoid it. Anyhow, as with everything in life, you just have to face the actuality in the end.

The woman's waters broke and flooded the mattress. I'd never thought the human body could contain so much liquid. As soon as they broke she cried and snatched at my hand even more fiercely, then lifted up her legs. She was exhausted but let them sink down again, and twisted herself into an awkward position.

'Hold on,' I said and with her daughter's help pulled off her skirt. I made the girl stay at her mother's head and keep on talking. I told her all would be well and I'd see to the baby. It didn't seem right for a little girl to see such a sight as birth so I knelt down and supported the woman's legs wide apart and waited.

I didn't have long to wait. First of all she bled a little and then to my horror, I thought her guts were showing, until I realised it was the head of the baby. For the only time during the whole birth I was frightened. What if the head could not get out? What should I do? Ought I to ease the head out?

Nature answered all my questions. With a great heave from the mother the head popped out and almost at once the entire tiny body slipped from the woman onto the soaking mattress.

No fear that the child might not be alive. A tremendous squeal quite terrifying in its intensity from something so tiny filled the van. The baby's pale arms beat the air and its monkey face creased up in fear and shock at the sudden entry into this uncomfortable world. For it must be uncomfortable, poor little devil, after having spent nine months in that nice, soft, mothering womb ... my sodden mattress would have been very unwelcoming.

In all the excitement I had not noticed the most important thing of all. The sex of the child. The little girl gave out a shout of joy and the woman wept with relief. It was a boy!

'Martha! Martha!' the woman cried to her daughter. 'A brother for you. After five daughters I have a son!'

The baby, still complete with afterbirth, was immediately cradled in her arms. She gazed at that adored son with a fierceness which would have laid down it's life for the child then and there. I had not fully realised the power of a mother's love until that moment.

'We'll have to cut the cord missus,' You couldn't have the baby trailing that bleeding mess around.

None of my knives would have been sharp enough to do the job without tearing too much, so in the end I used a razor blade, a rusty one into the bargain because I had no better. Of course I doused everything in the formula, even soaked the black cotton I used for tying off the end of the cord, all the while hoping and praying for the best. But there was such strength and power in that mother's love that I doubt a single germ would have dared attack her miraculous son.

We wrapped the baby in her skirt and after I'd cleaned her up as best I could I told the woman we'd better continue our journey to her village. With the little girl sitting beside me we found our way. Once off the Desert Road we followed a track till we reached the place.

What rejoicing greeted her! When she had left the village to visit her sick sister no one thought she might return with a young son. Still cradling the baby in her arms she was picked up and carried into her cottage. Aunts, cousins, nephews, nieces and neighbours crowded around her. Twice as large as life and very proud, her husband hovered around with a great grin on his face.

As I made to be off I was surrounded by these people, begging me to stay. They insisted that they had to clean up the van for me. They had to give me a meal. They had to give me a bed for the night. In no way could they consider me leaving them that night. And they were as good as their word.

The old van was washed and shined up inside and out. Then one of their own mattresses put in to replace my ruined one. All that evening a stream of people came in to wonder at the new baby and sit and talk to me as I ate my supper.

Australia ... Africa ... the showgrounds ... they couldn't hear enough of my life. When I took out the birds and played the fiddle they crowded round so close it was difficult to perform.

The whole village insisted I stayed with them for at least the next day and join in their sabbath. A sabbath on a Saturday? The only people I know who have that are the Jews and the Seventh Day Adventists but I said nothing and listened to their tale.

Chapter 12

The Legend of Te Kooti

People around those parts believed in the teachings of Te Kooti, a man whose creed had become a religion still followed to this day. He was exiled by the British to Chatham Island on a charge of gun running to the rebels, and while far away from his homeland he turned to religion and preached Hau Hauism, also known as the Pai Mire religion.

His followers chanted the words 'Haupa! Haupa! Hau! Hau!' which means, 'Pass Over', and was a magic cry to protect the people from the bullets of the British. The bullets would pass over their heads. He developed his own doctrine and called it Ringa-tu, which means 'The Upraised Hand' … that is part of the ritual.

I easily recognised many of the teachings as they were the same as my old Dad had often read from the Old Testament of the Bible. Ringa-tu is a mixture of The Book of Common Prayer, The Old Testament and certain Maori legends. They keep the sabbath on Saturdays, also celebrate the twelfth of the month and have a very hygienic set of rules regarding food. The first thing he did was to prohibit the eating of horseflesh.

Te Kooti wasn't the kind of man to remain exiled from his homeland, so he gathered his followers around him and told them to prepare to escape from Chatham Island. He ordered them to bind flax about their waists and be ready so that when the schooner arrived with provisions they could overpower their guards, without bloodshed, seize the ship and return to New Zealand. Upon no account should blood be spilt. Te Kooti considered he had been wrongfully banished. He wished to meet the British honourably and argue his case.

The ship *Rifleman* sailed in, and on the command of Te Kooti his followers rose up and overpowered their guards. He even had enough money to pay the captain to take them back to New Zealand.

They had barely left Chatham Island when a terrific storm arose. Waves forty feet high towered over the little ship and every time she wallowed in a trough the lightning flashed on the walls of water surging down on them. Those Maoris reckoned their last hour had come.

'Have faith!' cried Te Kooti. 'I have been betrayed. God has sent this tempest to destroy us. God must have a reason. I have failed in my covenant. One of us in this ship has sinned. Find the sinner!'

Panic stricken, they tried everything to appease their god. They threw overboard every single tiki and charm they had with them. If the sinner was not human then they must have an evil talisman with them. But all to no avail. The waves rose higher and higher and the ship became dangerously sluggish as water came over the sides and she didn't have time to right herself between the crashes of the waves on the deck. Looking around, Te Kooti noticed that one of his men was missing, and he became suspicious.

'Search him out!' he commanded. 'Bring that man to me.'

Soon they found the missing Maori huddled behind some casks, half dead with fear. When Te Kooti questioned the man he discovered he had disobeyed the commands and murdered his guard. Because of his evil act disaster would come to them all. Te Kooti ordered that the man be trussed up and thrown overboard. Immediately the seas subsided and the wind dropped so that they were able to sail for Gisborne without any more trouble.

But once ashore luck appeared to have deserted them. The British militia and the armed constabulary were in no mood for peace. They regarded Te Kooti as a renegade who should be hunted down with all possible speed. So began a life of wandering, sudden attack and outwitting his enemies until Te Kooti fled into the King Country in 1869.

On all his journeys Te Kooti was guided by the rainbow. The rainbow showed him many a time where to find the safe route ahead. Few people realise the importance of the rainbow. If you are starting out on a journey and you see it spanning the sky before you, then it is important to pause and wait and watch.

If the rainbow is bright in the positive hues of the spectrum, if you see red and orange in the ascendant then all is well. If the negative side, the blues and mauves are dominant, then you should ponder further and consider what might be amiss in your life. On no account should you proceed with your journey till the rainbow clears. Wait till it shifts. Not till the rainbow moves aside should you continue.

As soon as the British knew he had landed at Poverty Bay and was on the clifftop with his men they encircled the whole band of Maoris, but before night came on them a dense fog blew up from the sea and hid them from the view of the British. The soldiers were not concerned, because they could easily wait until daybreak for their attack. They settled down for the night, secure in the knowledge that their prey was marooned on the clifftop.

Te Kooti urged his followers to twist the flax they carried into ropes and in the dead of night they lowered themselves down the cliff and escaped. The next morning the British woke up and found the cliff deserted.

Te Kooti and his men led them a merry dance after that. With craft and cunning they outwitted their enemies at every turn, hoodwinking them by taking to the hilltops and marching round and round in circles so that the British imagined they were up against a huge army when it was only a handful of men. Each time the British closed in for attack a thick mist like the one which had saved them on the cliff descended and concealed them. When they wanted to know the safest route ahead they watched for the appearance of the rainbow and followed its directions.

The Maori band escaped into the Urewera Country, nearly eight hundred square miles of rocky mountain country bathed in mists and washed by continual rain. The landscape is mysterious, forever hazy and moist, and it would be easy to credit the existence of fairies and spirits in the Urewera Country. The local Tuhoe clan sheltered them from the soldiers; not that it was difficult because the country was so rugged they had all the natural advantages on their side. Up high are great tracts of primaeval forests. Ancient rimu and ratu trees rear up from the dense undergrowth. The Tuhoe had populated the entire countryside with fairies and the ghosts of their ancestors. Even the trees are people of Tane, and each tree has its own spirit.

Owls, parrots, bellbirds, fantails and the amazing morepork, whose call is just as its name is spelt, live in the forest. Lower down the slopes live the wild pigs, goats and deer. The land is a place of mystery, a perfect refuge for the fugitives with plenty of natural food to keep them alive.

Pursue him as they might, the British could not outwit Te Kooti. The Tuhoe warned him of the enemy's approach by calling on their conch shells from their eyries high up among the rocky crags. He would be for ever off and away again, eluding the soldiery.

Te Kooti was a fair minded man. He could not stomach injustice and considered the British had done him a great injury by banishing him from the country he loved so deeply. He demanded justice be done, and he set about tracking down the officers who had sentenced him to exile on Chatham Island years before.

One night, he and his followers descended upon Turanganui in the Gisborne area where troops were garrisoned and the two officers against whom he vowed vengeance were stationed. He managed to find only one of them but he shot and bayoneted the man and his entire family with the exception of one small child who ran off into the night. Then Te Kooti set about massacring the rest of the garrison. Over seventy people died that night.

The militia were after him in full cry after that. Late in 1869 he fought his last battle. In this final engagement of the Maori-Pakeha wars, one of his fingers was blown off and his side pierced, but he escaped. He fled into the country of the Kingites and devoted himself to the Ringa-tu church.

'Never fear,' he told his followers. 'The British are just and righteous. I shall be pardoned.'

This was the man who lived in the imagination of the people among who I found myself. Of course, the way you regard a hero depends upon who writes the history books. Many would say he was a wicked old Maori who deceived and tricked those who trusted him and engineered events to capture the imagination of ignorant natives. On the other hand, you could say he was a man of principle who sought to keep his people together by giving them a faith which could satisfy them. He could see that the encroaching Christianity was not enough to satisfy them, so he welded it together with their ancient myths and fables and gave them a reasonable working religion. He contrived to make the best of events at the time and keep the spirit of his people alive.

No one believed he would be pardoned, but he trusted the British and they must have respected him for, sure enough, in 1883 he was pardoned.

*   *   *

The family urged me to stay with them, they regarded my delivery of the boy child as nigh miraculous and were determined to keep me with their tribe. I could see they glanced at me with awe, although I knew I was merely a fortunate man and that events had played into my hands. Still, there seemed little point in arguing the point, throwing away a reputation that had fallen into my lap.

'Stay with us,' they begged. 'Teach us your healing ways. Teach us how you make a boy child by just telling a woman she is to bear a son.'

That needed straightening out for a start. I could get myself into a lot of strife if I started making such haphazard predictions, because my luck wouldn't hold out for ever.

'It is not given to humans to know whether their infants be sons or daughters,' I told them. 'Only occasionally is such a flash of knowledge granted ... only when there is need for the mother to have extra strength and faith. Such a flash of knowledge was granted to me on the Desert Road when your Evie was in such need. In the midst of fear and uncertainty the Spirit of the Unknown spoke to me, I was inspired, and so I gave your daughter confidence. To ask for more would be impertinent.'

They bowed their heads as they listened. 'Will you stay with us and teach us about the guiding Spirit?'

But I turned a deaf ear to their repeated requests that I stay longer. How could I? I'd got my living to earn. I stopped on for a couple of days but then it was time to go and I set off down the track with their good wishes ringing in my ears.

The rainbow arched dark and forbidding across the sky before I reached the main road. A tremor of fear went through me. I did not really believe the old tales but on the other hand the colours were so livid, the arc so strong, the rainbow really

134

appeared to bar my way. But I did not stop.

I turned onto the Desert Road and for a while forgot about the rainbow, but then I chanced to look up again and there it was. Close and menacing, it glowed in dark blues and greens against a stormy sky.

I passed a crowd of men standing by the roadside.

'Go back! Go back!' they cried. 'You are needed.'

How did they know I was needed? I'll never fathom it, but as I came to understand the Maoris over the years that followed I guess they had their own ways. Maybe it was a supernatural knowledge, or perhaps they were terrified of the rainbow like everyone thereabouts and would have prevented anyone from travelling towards it. I turned and drove back as fast as I could to the house where I'd been stopping.

'What has happened that I have been called back?'

The old grandmother of the family was standing, staring with unseeing eyes, in the doorway.

'Little Martha ... the daughter of Evie ... ' And she shook her head, her face creased with sorrow.

'She wasn't ill when I left.'

'She is drowned. She followed her sisters to the stream. They found her less than an hour ago.'

'Take me to her!'

A crowd of weeping, moaning women were gathered in Evie's hut. They sorrowed with the mother but they heaped their curses on me. The rainbow! I should have heeded the warning! I had brought disaster upon them. This was a day for evil matters and my careless action had brought tragedy upon them.

Despite my own feelings of disbelief I was very sorry, ashamed that I'd implanted the idea of my miraculous character in these simple peoples' minds and made myself appear responsible for their loss.

'Stand back! Let me see her.' I had to make a positive move.

The women fell away from the bed and I could see the child lying there. Her hair was limp and wet upon the pillow, her skin white as marble. She was so small and innocent that my heart turned over with sorrow at seeing such a dear little girl finished and done with before she'd known even a quarter of life's pleasures.

I remembered her so clearly sitting holding her mother's hand that day on the lonely Desert Road. She was too young to go yet. I stood and gazed at her motionless form, all the while feeling very guilty that I had driven off in the face of their ill omen.

As I gazed I had the feeling she was not quite still. Was there the faintest lift of the breast?

'Out of the way.' I pushed aside a couple of women who had returned to the bedside. I knelt beside her rubbing her hands and talking to her all the while. She was as still as death itself.

I placed my mouth over her lips and breathed into her and then pressed upon her thin chest. I listened with my ear to her heart, then I breathed into her again, holding her nose with my fingers. I pressed down upon her chest, again and again. All the time I prayed, begging the Spirit of the Unknown to come and help me in this hour of need.

As I knelt and prayed by the child and laid my ear close to her heart I swear I felt the flicker of a beat, but I said nothing. I never stopped breathing into her mouth and pressing upon her chest. Quite dizzy with the effort I almost passed out myself, the next thing I remember was eager hands shaking my shoulders.

'Look! Look!' they cried.

The child's head moved upon the pillow and next moment she was calling for her mother.

*　　　　　*　　　　　*

That event sealed my future in New Zealand. I had not chosen this path but, like so many avenues in my life, it chose me. From far and wide people flocked to see me. The word got around that I was a healer, a prophet, a man possessed of superhuman powers! The villagers now insisted that I stay with them longer and from all the neighbouring settlements they brought their sick and dying.

In many cases there is little you can do for a human who has tried medical aid and failed. If they've already been under the surgeon's knife there is absolutely nothing you can do. The rhythm of nature has been destroyed.

There are certain cases, though, where Faith can effect a

startling change in health. To effect this change you must get yourself in tune with the ways of those you are healing, learn the folklore, understand the deeply held convictions of the people you are curing. I set myself the task of learning as much as I could of the Maori way of life, absorbing and then translating the thoughts and ways into present day conditions.

Some of their ways are very wicked in our eyes, but when you realise it is not long ago they were fighting their wars and involved in tribal disputes among themselves, then they are more understandable.

I heard tell of a very snobbish British officer during the last war who was throwing his weight about, swanking away about his Highland ancestry, very proud of being half Scottish. A Maori standing nearby said quietly, 'Yes ... it's something we can both be proud of.'

'What do you mean?' demanded the Britisher, insulted since the Maori was as black as your hat.

'I have Scottish blood in my veins too.'

'You?'

'My grandfather used to eat them.'

They have a lovely sense of humour, but you've just got to judge them with care.

The people I was with told me of a captured chieftainess who their forebears had hypnotised. They made a hangi, which is a hole dug out of the ground filled with rocks. A huge fire was built on the rocks, and it was finally covered with a bed of leaves. They prepared the woman and laid her on the bed of leaves and then covered her with earth. Of course she came out of her hypnotic sleep but she could not get out of the hangi and she died. They cooked her well and truly and sent different parts of her body to the various chiefs in the area.

The more I knew of these people the more I became convinced that I could live a good, profitable life in the country, but on the other hand, I'd better look after myself very carefully.

The Maoris have a host of cures and remedies which are a necessity for them, living as many of them do in such isolated places. They taught me the use of karamu leaves. They showed me where to find them and how to gather them carefully at the right hour of the day, boil them for twenty minutes, then simmer them for an hour. The potion of the karamu leaf is used for sickness and trouble with the glands.

Then there is the wonderful Maori cure for internal and external bleeding. This is a very ancient remedy and was used by them in their wars. You gather the bark of a certain tree before dawn. When you have boiled it, strained it and reduced the liquid by a half again you are left with a potion which has the power to seal all wounds instantly.

Another shrub is the tutu. The ways of using that would take a lifetime to learn. I used the thick white syrup from its stalks to ease inflammation of the ovaries and bring down the swelling of the abdomen.

Not all the herbal medicines were remedies. They had more deadly uses too, and whereas in Australia the Aborigines work their vengeance by pointing the bone, or singing people to death, in New Zealand the ritual is called Marcuta. They help their magic along with the use of karaka berries. This berry is dried and powdered and then secretly slipped into the victim's food. Whoever eats it becomes paralysed and dies, yet there is no detectable sign of poison in the person while alive or in the body after death.

Once I fell foul of some people up beyond Rotorua and they attempted this method to get their own back on me. I felt so sick I couldn't move from the van. I swelled up inside and my liver appeared about to burst. The only way I survived was dosing myself with nux vomica and making myself sick as a dog.

Chapter 13

The Showgrounds of New Zealand

The new turn that life had taken caused me much thought. I'd come to the place because I wanted a change, and foreign ways are always interesting. But I'd arrived with no more thought of abandoning my show business and the little birds than taking off for the moon.

It isn't advisable to forsake all you know for your whole working life in pursuit of a new interest. People in their fifties often need a change, some say a change of job or a change of wife, but such ideas are really illusions. Nothing changes. We are as we were born, discontented creatures, fickle in our ways. The mere fact that when we reach our middle years we feel an urge for novelty should not blind our senses.

The smell of the tomb reaches us. We catch a whiff of death, we feel the hopeless desire to live again the years that have been wasted, we long for a brighter future.

How can the future be brighter after fifty? Our bodies are failing, our minds becoming absorbed with fears of our approaching end. Then the real worth of a human is apparent. Can they live with the evidence of their own mortality and still expand their thoughts? Can they settle for what they have been in the past? Can they look forward to what they will become without fear? Have they been content? Have they been charitable to others? Above all, have they lived up to the expectations of that really important person in their life ... themselves? For it is only in being true to yourself that you will finish your life contented.

If I deserted my old life I would not be true to myself. I would fling away all the old associations for a new set of exciting values and beliefs but I would never be more than a spectator among these strange people around me. Best to keep on with the old life and combine the two where possible. I'd remain a showman to the very end.

The shows over there were similar to those in Australia – mainly agricultural. Many towns and cities had two shows annually, a summer show and a winter one, and I never lacked for work.

The variety of acts wasn't as great as in Australia. I was a great novelty with my one-man act, but triumph always has it's reverse side and I found I excited a great deal of jealousy among the regulars. They got up to all manner of dirty tricks to keep me off the grounds, frighten me away, blacken my reputation. But they were no match for a bit of positive thought ... and action.

One time when I'd had a really big day at the Christchurch Show, and taken over a hundred and fifty pounds, I was checking the money afterwards with my helper. It was a sweltering hot day, and I just had a towel around me. We weren't too badly placed, we'd been given a little hut on the showground and it was cooler than the van or the tent. The other bloke went out to the toilet and when he was in there some chap came up demanding money. As he stood and argued a mob of fellows arrived and encircled him.

None of them was to know that this particular chap had been in the Olympics and was a champion boxer too, a fine, all round athlete. He laid into them, spread the first bloke's nose right across his face and then kept knocking them down as they came. After a taste of that medicine they ran off to fetch more of their mates and my helper staggered back to the hut where I'd quite unknowingly been counting the money.

'What's up mate?' He just slumped down in the corner. Grand fighter that he was he had had enough.

'They're out ... they're out ... to get me,' he gasped.

I snatched up my jungle knife and was off like a shot. Up the hill came a crowd of fellows but I wasn't waiting for them to get too close. Attack is always better than defence. Raising that jungle knife above my head I let out a howl of rage and charged straight down on them.

When my blood's up, it's really up. I'd take on an army. With my arms upraised the towel slipped from me. Stark naked I raced towards them with my flashing knife. I must have been a fearsome sight.

Instead of turning and running, their ranks parted and I found myself skidding through a crowd of startled faces.

'You bastards! You bastards! I'll show you! I'll teach you!' I could hear my shouts echoing around the empty showground.

'Hold on mister,' one of the lads called. 'We've done nothing' A couple of hands stretched out to prevent me wielding that knife.

They were just a bunch of lads looking for a mate of theirs! I'd got the wrong blokes. Did I look a fool! But they were real gentlemen. When they heard the reason for my attack they turned straight back down the hill and went looking for that bunch of dingoes who'd attacked my pal. I went back to the hut and left them to it.

'You right there Captain?' my mate asked.

'I fixed 'em proper,' I told him, wrapping the towel round me again. Well, in a certain fashion I had.

*　　　　　*　　　　　*

Pickpocket Fingers had the place next to me, and beside him was The Smallest Trotter in the World ... he was a real sham – a clipped Shetland colt pulling a tiny sulky. They told everyone that the colt was a seven-year-old horse. Sometimes the public deserves to be taken in; they don't trust the evidence of their own eyes.

People kid themselves all along the way. Those who want to believe in magic, the supernatural, ghosts and so on will find evidence of those things all around them. Those who are sceptical ... well, they'd still be sceptical if you handed them the Wizard of Oz on a plate.

Jasper the Invisible Ghost was a great draw for me. I did nearly as well with old Jasper as I did with The Electric Lady. I had a really creepy little show there ... but was the public satisfied? Not on your life. I reckon they'd not have been satisfied until they had the Holy Ghost himself sitting in their laps.

The whole act relies on the black art. It's not as sinister as it sounds. The art of the black cabinet came in the first place from Eastern Europe where it's still very popular. Every article on the stage is painted black, the showman wears black and a black mask, his step ladders are black and his chairs and boxes are black. The only items not black are the moving parts of the act which are painted with phosphorus paint. By clever manipulation coffins can open, nooses can dangle, hands come round doors, skeletons dance and bones rattle.

You'd think the public would be satisfied … but no. Foolishly, the first time I showed Jasper over there I put up a 'Money Back if Not Satisfied' notice. Quick as a flash after the show up comes a bloke, wife tagging along behind and a tribe of kids following.

'You stand by that?' he demanded, pointing at the notice. All that crowd of kids stared up at me as though I was some sort of criminal their brave dad was going to sort out.

'That's what it sez,' chipped in his wife for good measure. 'Money Back if Not Satisfied.'

'Ain't you satisfied?' I asked, rather cool.

'We never saw no ghost!' The man shouted and all the kids whinged in agreement. 'No ghost!'

'Shake yerself, yer silly dingbat,' I laughed because what else could I do but laugh. 'Haven't you read the notice properly? It's Jasper *the invisible* ghost. How can you see him if he's invisible?'

The man scratched his head and the dopey looking crowd of kids stared at him instead of me.

'Bloody bunch of crooks. What'd you expect off a showground,' the man muttered as they moved off.

Well I suppose if I'd had a great bunch of kids like that I'd be looking for some way of getting my money back.

Never put up a notice saying 'Money Back if Not Satisfied'. It really encourages the worst instincts in the public. Suggest to a person they may not be satisfied and they make a real meal of you.

At a show shortly afterwards I came across another sucker like me. Captain Davis was his name. He had a very nice manner, was a civil sort of a bloke and owned a lion called Arthur. Captain Davis was a strong family man. His wife helped him with his act, his eldest son called them in, and besides that he had several little kiddies and a baby too. The baby was always in its pram outside. The Davises were a really nice showground family.

And Arthur was an exceptional lion – more like the family pet. He'd curl up and sleep on command, jump through a hoop, let one of the kids tie on a bonnet and open his mouth so Captain Davis could stick his head in. Just a single lion, which was rather an unusual act.

'Money Back if Not Satisfied' the notice read outside. I remember that clearly.

One man came stamping up after the show, very belligerent. 'Seen better at the Punch and Judy,' he sneered.

'What's wrong Sir?' Captain Davis asked.

'Bloody lion didn't bite yer bloody head off. Bloody waste of money.'

We have to deal with some very coarse people. They seem to think we're standing there like a load of dummies just waiting to take the knocks. I reckon poor Captain Davis was too much of a gentleman for our kind of life. He'd have been handing the money back half the time.

There was no fear that Arthur would ever take his head off; he had nothing to worry about from that lion. But a couple of months later I heard that one of the camels on the showground came over and bit the baby's head off as it lay in its pram. Strange fact that. Some people have the worst luck in the world and often it's the nicest and straightest ones who go under in my particular game.

At the Hamilton Winter Show the other showmen got together and wanted me off the place. I was too great an attraction.

'Give Captain Lloyd an empty tent and he'd fill it in two minutes,' I've heard it said.

That was because I was not ignorant like them. I'd studied human nature. I could talk and hold people's attention, play the fiddle and the harp and perform with the birds. With The Flying Birdcage and The Indian Ropetrick I could keep a whole crowd interested. Even if I didn't have The Electric Lady and those other acts I'd still have managed, all on my own.

This particular time at Hamilton the others weren't game to compete against me. They'd been to the Secretary of the Show before I'd got settled in and told him I was a bad character. A loose and dishonest man.

'You'd believe this rabble?' I asked him. I chose my words carefully. I wasn't going to resort to the ignorant speech of those around me.

'You'd better get off the ground,' he told me. He could not look me in the eye, though.

'Filthy gossip and lies! A man of your education and

knowledge should understand the ways of the ignorant.' I told him straight what I thought. 'Why, when I was Ringmaster of Pagel's Circus in Africa I handled my performers better than this. Do I look like the class of man who'd steal and live off women?'

He shook his head undecidedly. By the time I'd told him about my reputation in Australia, shown him my posters, explained about the type of person who would want me out of the way, he was halfway to agreeing with me.

'Which of these men can play the fiddle, entertain a crowd with wholesome family fare? ... why, when I was Ringmaster at Taronga Park Zoo I'd never have had these fellows on the ... '

'You were Ringmaster at Taronga Park?'

That did it. He ordered that those other dingoes strike their tents that instant. I was given the pick of the sites and after that they were allowed to pitch their tents again.

Public relations are very important. You've got to present a respectable show. Stands to reason no one is going to let their kids come and watch you if you aren't a decent sort of person. True, you can get by with the passing crowd, who are out for a thrill and a bit of a shock. But let the strip shows and such take care of them. The farthest I'd go in that direction was The Girl in The Fishbowl. Admittedly, she did a bit of stripping, but strictly controlled under my supervision and the show was aimed more to mystify people than to pander. That tiny lady dancing in the fishbowl was very intriguing.

A good family entertainment is much more in my line and I always found it better to aim at the best class of people rather than the lowest. It's the same as with life itself; mixing with ignorant people is no pleasure at all. I could always get on well with educated people, even if I'm not what you'd call a scholar myself. I respect knowledge and good manners. I respect a good class of person.

I hadn't seen the end of the dingoes at that Hamilton Show, though. My enemies were very tenacious people, and they wanted me off the showground. One night as I was packing up by myself in the tent, I heard my little Ruby whine. A clever little dog, she loved people, loved the crowds and the children, but she could never abide anyone sneaking about outside the tent.

'What's up girl?' I asked. Her hackles were rising along her spine and her lip curled back baring her teeth. 'You go and see 'em off, old girl,' I said, and as soon as I undid her chain she shot into the darkness.

Immediately a squeal tore through the night air, then another squeal and a yelp followed by a thud. I threw myself out after her and there, in front of the tent, was a knot of men. One of them had kicked the dog and she was standing there, paw bent back and head down, gathering up strength to have another go.

'Leave off Ruby! Leave 'em to me!' I was beside the animal in a trice stroking her neck. 'Which of you kicked this dog?'

They laughed. I suppose seven of them felt they could afford to have a good laugh at me. All on my own, no mate nearby. Besides Ruby there were the little birds and another young dog I'd taken on. It didn't take two seconds for the possibility to flash through my mind of what they might get up to with the animals and the gear.

Out from the bunch came a hefty young Coconut. Coconuts are what the Maoris call the Islanders. He wasn't much in height, about the same as me, and I'd say he matched me in the rest of his measurements.

'What you asked old man?' He laughed and threw his head back.

He had lovely strong white teeth that were a credit to him. I reckoned they were too good to let him keep in that nasty grinning mouth.

The others crowded behind him, in for the kill. I stepped back, but there wasn't much else I could do. Poor Ruby put her tail down but she didn't run. She faced them, her teeth still bared.

'C'mon ... let's be having yer!' I yelled. What else could I do?

'Get that bitch!' one shouted. 'Get his bitch ... '

My blood ran cold for a brief moment as I thought of my defenceless animals. They were my responsibility. I could not fail them.

'You want what's coming to you before the bitch? Eh old man?'

That lousy Coconut came towards me, one foot already on the mat outside the tent.

I dived down at the speed of lightning before he guessed my intention. I flicked the mat from under his feet and sent him crashing. Before his mates had time to take action I was on him.

I grabbed one leg and with all my strength – just about the last scrap I could summon up – I swung him off the ground.

I got him in a Japanese leghold. Then I went for them. I swung that Coconut round and round. His stupid mates just stood there. One moment their leader had been menacing me, the next moment he was swinging around in front of them. They were too slow to get out of the way. His head knocked into their knees and the ones who did not run off tumbled to the ground like ninepins.

One last swing and I let go. That Coconut ended up in a heap under the paydesk. Quick as a flash I was in and out of the tent. I stood over him with a tent peg.

'Want any more of that? Want any more? Plenty where that came from!'

Only groans came from them. The Coconut was rubbing his head and his mates feeling for broken bones.

'Get goin' in one second flat! I can hear me mates coming and they're better fighters than me. They don't breed fighters like us Aussies over here ... you'd best remember that!'

They didn't stop to argue. They'd had a good demonstration of the art of self preservation. My hands were shaking as I bandaged Ruby's paw, and I reckon I'd just about reached my limit.

*   *   *

Just looking after yourself is a lonely business, and as the years caught up with me I wanted some more company. That was when I married for the second time. It was a Maori style marriage, just her father reckoning on it being a good idea. No more than his consent was needed and soon we were nicely set up together. She didn't take to shifting around any more than Rose had done. She liked to stop with her people and live among those she knew. That was their way of life and I could not persuade her to come around the showgrounds with me, but over the years I always returned to her, always helped out when I could. We had seven children, lovely strong kids, every one of them a credit. If anyone ever asks what are the best things in life

I'd say ... it's your children. Even if you hardly ever see them you know they're there, carrying on in the future and taking along a little bit of you with them.

About that time young Lola got herself truly into trouble. She'd been inclined to head off from time to time and just come back when she got sick of a bloke. It came to the point of the bloke in question doing the disappearing act and Lola came to me three months gone. She wanted medicine to shift the baby but I wasn't having any. That's a dangerous thing to play with. I thought she'd decided to keep the kid and gave the matter no more thought till a week or so later when I called round to pay her some money I owed. The door was opened by a wrinkled old woman with a face like a hawk.

'Ssh ... you can come back later. She ain't herself right now.'

I pushed past and there was Lola lying on the bed, with only a woollen cover over her breast and stomach and the abortionist's instruments laid out on the table by the bed. I didn't ask any questions. I tipped the lot on the floor and told that old woman to get going.

Lola had the baby, settled in with a homosexual man who ran a rifle range and I reckon she was a lot safer there.

Chapter 14

More Healing and More Girls in my Fishbowl

Outside the Show gets the Dough! A very old, very true saying. The Archangel Gabriel and all his angels could be playing their trumpets inside, but if there isn't a good spruiker calling them in you'd have an empty tent.

Every year Dave paid my air fare so that I would be able to help him at the Sydney and Melbourne Shows.

'You're the best spruiker in the business, Owen. You're worth thousands to me. There's no one can shout for the pygmies like you.'

'IT'S UBANGI ... YOU BETCHA!' I'd holler. 'Come and see the strange people from darkest Africa, the land of wonder and mystery.'

People would pause and listen for a moment. They'd hover first, not sure whether to move off or come inside and see what all the excitement was about. Their hands would slip towards their pockets. I'd won!

'Every evening at the setting of the sun Ubangi pays homage to the Giant Elephant! Come and see the Sons and Daughters of the Sacred Tiny People! Shake hands with Solomon. Solomon is the direct descendant of King Solomon and The Queen of Sheba. Step Up! Step Up! Step up and see the Dance of the Pygmy Virgins!'

Once I'd got the crowd started they'd flock in from early morning till late at night. Hour after hour, day after day until I was glad when showtime was finished and I could spend a few days with my parents before catching the plane back to Auckland.

My life became even busier in New Zealand than it had been in Australia, and I began to feel the weariness that comes with age. My reputation as a healer went ahead of me wherever I travelled, and people visited me in every place I stopped. They came from far and near, in trucks, on horseback, on foot. Often

I would be treating them well into the night because I always had to finish my show first.

Word of my cures spread about the country and my fame became a sore embarrassment. Instead of coming to see me perform they were coming to be healed. I'd have them waiting outside the tent twenty deep, and each one needing careful attention.

'A sorcerer is amongst ye!' The churches began to take notice, and although I never heard the sermon myself I did hear I was being preached against from the pulpit.

'A man who trades with the Devil and practices his evil ways. Shun! Spurn! Deny him or ye shall be enmeshed in the net of Beelzebub!' Some of their expressions were very primitive.

Healing is a wonderful, uplifting experience. A time when you come into contact with the most basic elements of a human being and at the same moment receive grace from The Spirit of the Unknown. If those who spoke against me from the security of their cloth had moved among the simple folk like I did, they wouldn't have thought so badly of me. No harm came from my actions. Many were those who could not be helped, but they went on their way more content souls because care and attention had been shown them. If you sow only good, positive thoughts, then you will reap the same in results. Life has a sure way of equalising the payment for your deeds.

Let the Church care for those who follow its teachings ... but let it stop meddling with those who interpret The Spirit of the Unknown in their own fashion. Many a good person has been stifled with doctrine and ritual, many a person who saw the way straight and true has been confused with too much strait-laced teaching.

People have forgotten about wisdom these days ... there's a lot of ignorance in the world, even among the high up. Ignorance is the worst sin in life. Some people you can't really blame for their conditions – maybe they never had a chance – but even unschooled people can have wisdom, commonsense and judgement.

Many people are ignorant because they just can't be bothered to learn the rights and wrongs of life. Some of the most learned folk are the most ignorant of all because they have become blinded by the power of their book learning. They don't look at life and see what it's really all about. They ignore the evidence of their eyes and make sweeping judgements on the rest of humanity. They sum up situations without standing back and considering for a while, label people haphazardly and don't take account of the asset side as well as the debit.

I had a couple of lesbians working for me at Invercargill. They'd been down there at a lesbian convention and needed some ready cash to get home again.

'Mind a bit of stripping?' It was all the work I could offer when they came round the showground looking for work.

Truth to tell, I wasn't very happy at the thought of women like that around. I didn't know what they might get up to.

'Means nothing to me,' one of them replied. 'If the money's good why should I bother what I do?'

Her mate didn't feel the same though, and was more shy.

'I need someone in the Fishbowl. Pay's good.'

They argued between themselves and finally agreed. They'd take turns in the Fishbowl.

They looked at me a bit suspiciously. I swear they thought I was up to no good, having a rockbottom opinion of men. The truth was I'd no intentions in that direction. Lesbians can be tricky women and I wondered to myself if I'd done a sensible thing.

Those two girls worked like Trojans. One in the Bowl, the other out of it, taking turns non-stop. When they weren't performing they'd come and give me a hand with anything they could tackle. They were really good women.

About that time I caught the 'flu and went down really crook, which is a dangerous situation for a man on his own like me. I'd no one to help out, no mate to trust. It meant dragging myself around to see to the tent, the animals and still try to keep the money rolling in as best I could.

'You ought to have more sense in your head than this, Captain Lloyd,' one of them said to me when she found me struggling up from my mattress to see to some banners that had flapped loose. I was moving as fast as I could before the next wave of fever sent me sweating and shivering back to the blankets.

'You stop where you are. Want a cup of tea?' I could only shake my head as her mate covered me up and refilled my mug with water.

Those two women took over. They managed The Fishbowl and Jasper too. I was not a penny short, not a thing went missing. Really good women, and if people like to go around the world saying nasty things about lesbians then I'd suggest they cause a lot less trouble in life than those who function in the conventional fashion.

The Fishbowl dance could be very taxing on the performer, especially if the weather was hot, because intense lighting was needed for the lens to throw the image. Some times of the year the girls fairly cooked.

Up in Auckland I had an American Negress, as black as the ace of spades. She nearly went mad with the heat. I'd been busy with Jasper when I saw a great crowd around the Fishbowl, struggling and pushing to get a good look. Scared that they'd damage the set-up, I raced over. There was my Negress running with sweat, dancing around in her birthday suit. I flung a cloth over the bowl and leapt into the van.

'Whadderyer think yer doin?' I demanded.

She couldn't reply, poor girl, she was sweating like a pig and quite breathless.

'They'll have us off the ground if they see those kinds of goings on. I'll be ruined!'

True enough, inside five minutes the other showmen had the secretary over at my tent warning me off. A fine kettle of fish! I apologised of course and tried to explain. Finally he let me stay if I didn't exhibit the Fishbowl again.

I took the girl, tipped a bucket of cold water over her and got her to dry herself off. With a lace shawl round her head she looked like a black spider when her skinny arms poked out ... but very exotic with it. I set her to telling fortunes and the money rolled in nearly as well as with the Fishbowl.

A Samoan Jew named Samantha was the best looking girl I ever had. She was very tall and coffee coloured with skin like velvet. I had to watch her though, she'd get carried away with herself even if it wasn't very hot. Off would come the very last stitch and I'd have to belt round to the van and kill the lights double quick.

'I've got nothin' to be ashamed of,' she'd pout, very annoyed at my interference.

'Never said you had. Got to think of my reputation, like I

keep telling yer.'

'Back home they like their money's worth,' she'd argue.

'Ever heard of doing in Rome what the Romans do? They aren't like 'back home' here. They like their sex respectable.'

She didn't mean to make a nuisance of herself, but had an artistic temperament and forgot what she was up to. One night I wandered over to the Bowl to have a stickybeak and got the shock of my life. There was a man in there with her trying to get fresh.

I had to cover up the Bowl quickly and get over to the van and sort him out.

Of course you came across all sorts. Sometimes I'd be fortunate and find a very nice class of person to assist. At one ground I'd been quite unable to find a girl to strip for me so, I'd just asked among the crowd.

'I'm not very good looking and I'm rather old, but I hope I'll give satisfaction,' one elderly Maori woman told me very shyly.

'Don't you worry dear,' I said. 'Just give us a nice dance and we'll be happy.' I was very relieved to find anyone who would oblige.

I was shocked when I looked into the Bowl. Her breasts hung down like strips of leather and as she moved they spun around with a life of their own. It was more like a tassel dance, you might say.

She'll never get them in, I thought. But she was intent on doing her best and to my amazement a huge crowd gathered to watch. Those sinewy arms and skinny breasts fascinated them. I showed her for two more nights and she made more money for me than ever my sexy Samoan or my Negress.

Another Maori who did very well was Annie. She was an inventive woman who gave them a good run for their money. She painted herself up with silver paint until she looked like a creature from outer space, and then got up on a table and did a very provocative dance up there. She gave herself pneumonia in the end. The silver paint clogged her pores and made her really crook.

Gigi was one of the best girls I ever had. She was very capable of looking after herself too. She'd been a professional stripper and took no cheek beyond what she wanted. She gave as good as she got.

Gigi was a very provocative girl. She was at her best with The Electric Lady, and she'd get the crowd roaring when she lit the neon tube up with a touch of her fingers. What she really enjoyed doing was bending over in her grass skirt and getting the chaps all worked up so they'd try and pinch her bottom. The moment their fingers came near, sparks flew from her flesh and they'd burn their fingers. How she'd laugh at them!

Working with women has lots of difficulties. The women are usually nice, decent people making their money as best they can, but it's the class of men they attract that's the trouble. Dealing with crude men can be a real headache. As the years rolled by I realised, of course, that the men were getting far younger than me and I was no longer at my peak when it came to sorting them out.

*   *   *

New Zealand soon kept me as busy as Australia had done. I followed a similar trail to my old one back home. After Hastings Summer Show in October, I'd move on to Martin, Danneverk, Palmerston North, then down to Wellington to catch the overnight ferry to the South Island.

I'd start at Christchurch then on to Ashburton, Timaru, Omaru, Dunedin, Invercargill and back to Christchurch. Next there was the ferry back to Wellington and I would travel up to Rotorua for the Christmas Carnival and on to Whakitane, Opetiki, Gisborne, Warioa, Wanganui and up to Hamilton for the Winter Show. Then I'd carry on back through Wantageri, New Plymouth and Wanganui.

The sick, like the poor, are always with us, and wherever I stopped people besieged me with all manner of requests to heal the afflicted. People called around at the tent for treatment and I'd still be dealing with them well into the night.

'Are you the man who can cast out The Devil?' I was asked one day by a very distressed woman.

'I've no truck with The Devil.'

'The church says that you deal with The Devil.'

Certainly they'd said some very nasty things about me and my devilish practices, but I'd not given them much thought. It was enough to make a cat laugh really. The Church doing my advertising for me!

'Will you come and help my family? Come, please come, or we shall all die.'

'Your whole family?'

'My sister died last month. We were all at her funeral and the requiem mass was being sung for her soul ... poor dear, she died mad and demented. As we sang my brother fell to the floor and froth came from his mouth. The spirit had left our sister's body, and flown from the coffin straight into our brother.'

'Is he still possessed?'

'He has been taken by the same evil spirit. He died raving within two weeks and the spirit has now passed into my daughter.

'How d'you mean?'

'At the hour of his death she fell mad. She screamed and howled like a dog and clawed at us as though she would kill us. Come! You must come! The evil spirit is within her and even if she dies, which would be a release for her, the spirit will come in to another of us.'

I followed the woman to her house in Palmerston North, and sure enough, from the screams I could hear as we approached, the girl was mad, all right.

'Leave her with me,' I told them, and opened the door of the room where they kept her.

A howling figure hurled itself at the door and she'd have slammed it shut if my boot had not been in the way. The sight of her chilled me more than her cries or lamentations.

Scraps of straw and excreta clung to her hair and face. Blood from great scratches was smeared down her arms and congealed on both wrists and the backs of her hands. She reeked of urine and the stink of a thousand cats hung about her. That savage creature snatched at my hand and tried to drag me in. Frenzied with frustration when she could not get hold of me, she rolled herself in a ball and spat with fury.

'Come out mister,' the family called. 'Come out, she'll turn on you.'

Great tears began to roll down her face and the spitting stopped as her body was convulsed with sobbing. Somewhere inside that crazed monster was a gentle human soul which was breaking its heart at the cruel mesh of madness which snared it. She had become a beast and in that condition could fasten her teeth into my throat and kill at a bite.

'Bring her to me at Popaki,' I told them.

Four huge Maoris were needed to secure her, great six footers. They got her in the back of a truck and held her down. They brought her to the hut where I was stopping on the shores of Lake Rothira.

Lake Rothira is fed from the icy streams that flow off the volcano Ngarahoe. The atmosphere surrounding the snowy peak and the clear, freezing water of the lake speaks of icy purity and cleanliness.

First of all we put her in an outhouse but she began to tear it apart. She pulled out a six inch nail from the timbers with the ease of taking a pin from a pin cushion. No room or hut was sturdy enough to secure her, so we rolled her up in a length of canvas and kept our vigil by that poor demented creature all night.

At first light I told the Maoris to carry her down to the lake and I followed them. In my heart I was confident that the spirit causing such trouble would not be able to survive the pure environment of Lake Rothira. The rising sun tinged the snow covered cone of the volcano with pinks and oranges and the most delicate hint of blue turning to mauve. All was harmony, beauty and purity.

'Immerse the woman in the waters,' I told them.

They unwrapped her from the canvas and waded into the lake with her.

'Keep her under, right under till I say.'

Choking and spluttering they pulled her out after half a minute.

'And again!' I ordered.

Five more times they immersed that girl in the waters of Lake Rothira and each time she came up gasping and choking and a trace weaker on each successive occasion.

'Leave her go and stand aside,' I told them finally and they laid her on the lakeside and stood back.

'The Spirit of the Unknown has driven the evil from your mind. The waters of the lake have washed away the filth from your body. See! You are as spotless as on the day you were born.

Get up and walk back to the hut with me.'

The girl staggered to her feet. Meek as a lamb she took hold of my hand and together we walked away like a couple of lifelong friends.

Chapter 15

Potions, Poultices, Dreams and Omens

The power of the mind is a tremendous ally when dealing with the forces of evil. Not everyone can recognise its strength. The innermost recesses of the brain hold the key to many illnesses – people convince themselves of their sickness and then exhibit all the symptoms. If the healer can reach those deeply hidden convictions and work to nullify their power at the source, that's when many a cure can be effected.

The power of the mind combined with certain commonsense remedies was what most humans had to depend on over the centuries, and in certain isolated parts of the world that is still the only hope in time of illness.

I've cleaned many gangrenous wounds with the application of a sheep's paunch to the affected part. It simply needed a good, fresh paunch, not cleaned, tied around the wound. In forty-eight hours time all the gangrene would have been eaten away and the area cleaned. The putrefying matter in the paunch feeds upon the gangrene and absorbs it. Putrefaction cannot live on healthy flesh, so the undamaged area behind the wound is freed of its harmful neighbouring cells and left clean. The rottenness of the paunch feeds upon the rottenness of the wound.

One of the best poultices in the world came from Grandfather Davies, who had it in turn from Mrs Srecks, who'd had it from a Chinese grocer out on the diggings in Ballarat. Mr Srecks had a tumour on his liver and no one could operate on the man. The Chinaman came to her when he heard of the tragedy and told her to take a bowl and into it place a mixture of breadcrumbs, grated Sunlight soap, sugar and a tablespoonful of washing soda in hot water, the same of boracic acid ... adding some eucalyptus oil if it was handy.

'Spread poultice on poor man's belly. Over where liver is. Cover with a lily leaf,' the Chinaman told Mrs Srecks. Many people have to make do with a cabbage leaf but a lily leaf is better.

On the third day Mrs Srecks saw a livid mark on her husband's stomach, on the fourth day the tumour burst and the poison drained away. To this day Srecks' Poultice is used around Ballarat.

Cures to our ailments are often at hand if we can only recognise them. Most times we're rushing about our business with too much speed and have too little patience to try simple remedies. In those situations The Spirit of the Unknown cannot communicate, but when sleep comes and the defences are lowered, enlightenment may be given to us. Many times I've seen the way ahead through dreams when ordinary thinking has failed.

A young woman was brought into my tent one day. Her husband had transported her in the back of his truck on a straw mattress.

'Bring her in,' I told them. A showground tent wasn't the best place for a groaning woman but I'd finished for the night.

'What's the matter, my dear?' I asked, but she only groaned and clutched at my hand.

'She has a terrible pain in her belly,' her husband whispered and when he lifted off the blanket I could see her stomach was swollen like a balloon.

I shrank from getting involved with her. Whatever the trouble was she had left it very late to find help. She winced with pain as I gently explored the swelling.

'The centre of the swelling is in her ovaries and it has spread into her womb. Why haven't you found help before?' I demanded.

'She's had this pain before but never so bad. Each time I say we must go to the hospital but she's scared they'll take her womb away from her. She's frightened of you too, but she knows you can't take her womb away.'

'She must go to the hospital first thing tomorrow. Her sickness has gone too far for me,' I told them. 'But tonight we'll make her as comfortable as possible here in the tent.'

That night I dreamed and the dream was as vivid as life itself. All around me were great shrubs and on the ground a pile of the shrubs' branches. Pale green leaves with woody stalks were leaking white sap. I saw the shrub being thrown by unknown hands into a pot and a fire lit and the stream rising from the vessel. Then the potion was strained and poured into an earthenware crock and placed in the running water of a stream to cool it off quickly.

In that dream I watched those hands rub the liquid all over the girl's abdomen and then raise her head and give her a draught of the same liquid. Then she lay back and the dream faded.

First thing next morning I was out looking for the shrub. All around the fairground was heath and scrub, and the bush I'd seen in my dream was in great abundance. I gathered three boxes of twigs and leaves and took them back to the van.

I followed what I had seen in the dream to the smallest detail, even putting the liquid in the earthenware jug and cooling it in running water.

'This is the cure for your woman,' I told the man. Between us we washed her in the liquid and urged her to sip the juice slowly from a cup. We moved her into a hut where she could rest peacefully all day and at regular intervals I instructed the man to repeat the whole process.

'I'm easier,' she whispered to us that night. By next morning her stomach had flattened out and the next day they were on their way home again, marvelling at the speed of the cure.

All through history dreams have been studied and analysed. When Pharoah saw the seven thin cows devour the seven fat ones in his dream, when he saw the seven ears of corn blasted with the east wind and consume the seven good ones, he knew he was on to something. But he was a worldly man and needed a simple dreamer, like Joseph, to interpret the meaning.

The closer we remain to nature the more in tune we are with natural events. Time is all around us. Past, present and future surround us and we are spinning particles of humanity. The simplest among us have not built up barriers of material needs to blunt our sensibilities. When simple people collide with the past we know how to accept the portents and adjust our lives accordingly.

The tragedy of Tangiwai had been foretold eighty years earlier by Te Fiti, the Maori spiritual leader of the day.

'Tangiwai, I name this place Tangiwai!' His followers listened as they all stood by the creek at the foot of Mount Ruahpehu.

They whispered the name 'Tangiwai' amongst themselves,

which means in Maori, 'A Place of Crying in the Waters.'

'An important visitor will come to our shores and on the eve of their arrival there will be heard a crying in the waters of this place.'

In 1953 The Queen visited New Zealand and people crowded to see her from far and near. Heavy rains had fallen the day before and the crater lake of Mount Ruahpehu was full. During the night part of the side fell away and the waters flooded down the volcano carrying away the railway bridge.

Next morning the trainful of people coming to welcome the Queen came along the track. No one knew the bridge had gone. Within seconds the entire train plunged into the waters below and the prophecy was fulfilled.

*   *   *

The Maoris were disappointed that the Queen would not be visiting their King upon her visit for they still regard their King with pride. I had a dream several months before she came, and in that dream I saw the Queen sitting talking to King Koreki in his palace at Narawakia. When I told the Maori chief at Rotahiti about my dream he shook his head in disbelief.

'She will not come to King Koroki, we have been told it will not be so.'

'You may have been told by the officials but my dream showed that she will come,' I told him. 'We must use our will to bring this about.'

'But it's not on her journey. We've been told it's not on her journey.'

As soon as word got round about my dream, King Koroki called the Maori chiefs to a banquet at his palace. A mass of people surrounded the palace when we arrived.

'We have come to speak of the Queen's visit to your King,' I told them.

'We shall eat first and talk afterwards,' the most senior chief replied.

Out of the hangi they brought turkey, sucking pig, fowl and meat of all kinds with piles of kumera, their type of sweet potato. Besides the cooked meats there were all varieties of shellfish,

160

river fish, raw abalone and eels.

I took care what I ate. The Maoris love their fish stinking, they'd leave the crayfish and the pippies in water till they were green and putrid and the more maggots crawling about inside the flesh the sweeter they reckoned it to be. It was the same with corn, another favourite of theirs. They left it till it was rotten then pummelled and boiled it. The smell was indescribable, and I reckoned a few helpings of that would have finished me off. I felt safest eating meat boiled with sowthistle, because nothing much could go amiss with a simple dish like that.

When we had eaten and drunk one of the chiefs addressed the King. He told him that he should contact the Queen personally and override the Government's decision. The Maoris argued among themselves. They were worried that this might cause trouble with the Government so I got up and asked for permission to address the elders and chiefs directly.

'I know what is going through your minds,' I told them. 'You are thinking, what business is it of his? He is a pakeha. This is Maori business.' They murmured among themselves.

'I had a dream and in that dream I saw the Queen sitting among you.'

A great sigh of satisfaction filled the room. 'As I said, you are wondering what I, a pakeha, is doing speaking to you in your own Meeting House. I must tell you that I have lived among you for the last ten years. Your desires are my desires, your honour is my honour, and this is a matter of the honour of our great King Koroki.'

They grunted and clapped and cheered among themselves.

'What shall we do?' one of the chiefs asked. 'The Government says she will not visit our village.'

'If you give me permission to act on your behalf I will go to Auckland and see the officials who are arranging Her Majesty's visit.'

'Go then, and bring back the news whether it be good or bad,' I was told.

I hurried up to Auckland and saw the officials dealing with the visit of Her Majesty.

I was completely unsuccessful. The Queen was not to visit King Koroki and that was the end of it. Her itinerary had been organised months before and I was given the impression that I was a foolish meddler and they could not wait for me to get out of their offices.

Next morning I went to *The Star* newspaper and asked to see the editor on extremely urgent and confidential business that could be discussed with none other.

He listened to me very civilly and then pointed out that there was nothing he could do in his newspaper, but he came up with a very sensible suggestion.

'Why don't you try another avenue of approach entirely? Queen Elizabeth will be visiting Queen Salote in Tonga. Now Queen Salote's son is in New Zealand. I know him slightly. If you wrote a letter for him to give to his mother then she might speak to the Queen for you.'

I knew I had found the way. I knew Her Majesty would visit King Koroki now. Events only needed to be set in their proper motion and all would be resolved. Inside a week the letter was in the hands of Queen Salote.

Queen Elizabeth had an outstanding time in Tonga. Queen Salote was a charming lady. She had caught the imagination of the British during the Coronation, when the papers all said she was the most feted head of state to attend. A big woman with a lovely smile and a warm heart, she was so natural that everyone took to her immediately.

She had laid on a right royal turn-out for Queen Elizabeth, and Her Majesty enjoyed herself so much she asked Queen Salote if she had any wish she would like to make.

'I have a request, but it is a delicate matter,' Queen Salote told her and handed her the letter from King Koroki.

The upshot was that the Maori King was contacted and told that the Queen would pass by his village where the elders might gather as a welcoming gesture. Obviously the officials had managed to get themselves in the act and water things down, but it was better than nothing.

The excitement! The rejoicing! They'd never known such an occasion as that.

Days before she came they were in a frenzy preparing their village for a grand reception. Garlands of flowers and bunting and flags were hung everywhere and the whole approach was lined with palms ... an avenue of palms grew up overnight. The

Maoris just dived off into the bush and dug up all the available trees and replanted them along the road.

The Queen certainly didn't just 'pass by' as the officials had predicted. She was most tactful too; before her car entered the village she had the royal standard removed from the bonnet so as not to offend their king. She was a real lady, sensitive to the feelings of others in every way.

She was welcomed by King Koroki, and although none of the officials had planned it, she accompanied him to the Meeting House where tea was laid out and afterwards the whole party watched the Maori warriors streaming down the river Wakaito in their war canoes in her honour.

I'll never see such a sight again. The cheering, the chanting and the joy of all those around her was overwhelming. Queen Elizabeth had the greatest welcome of all in King Koroki's village, and it was two hours before she was on her way again.

Chapter 16

Home Again

It was a real wrench leaving New Zealand. I'd been very happy there but the old people back home weren't getting any younger. Not having a settled home and all the travelling, and then sometimes having to deal with a low class of person that didn't respect anything but the power they could pack behind their punches, meant I was beginning to feel my own age too.

Mother and Dad had been wonderful to me. Over the years they'd kept the home fires burning. I'd been able to leave my gear and animals with them whenever I wanted a trip, and when I got back there was always a welcome. I couldn't let them finish their days without a bit of return, could I?

I reckon I got back to Melbourne just in time. Mother died not long after and Dad followed her within a fortnight. That was the blackest time of my life. Mother, Dad and Dave were the best friends I ever had. Dave died not long afterwards, and when he'd gone I lost all interest in the show world.

Showpeople can finish their lives in very comfortable situations or quite the opposite. I've seen it all. There are families who keep on going as a big group and the young ones carry on so the old ones always have a niche in the business. Then there are the businessmen like Dave who invest and make provision for themselves and their dependents.

What worried me was the way the majority ended up. Their acts became grubbier and less professional and the young ones on the ground soon ripped them off. I never wanted to look pathetic. I needed a new direction.

It took some time to settle down after all my travels. First I attempted to pick up the threads in Melbourne and tried to look up old mates, but many had moved off or just handed in their chips and died. I found that depressing. Some say you should never go back to your old haunts and I reckon that's very true.

So I made the break. Packed up my belongings, loaded the birds and old Ruby in the back of my van and went off up to Sydney. I'd always loved the bright lights and the bustle up there. I found myself a nice little shop in the Botany Road where I could deal in old wares and I spent my nights up at The Cross entertaining by the El Alamein Fountain. I never felt lonely that way. People were always dropping in at the shop during the day and at night there were the crowds on the street to chat to and have a joke with. Everyone who passed by stopped to listen to the fiddle and watch the birds. I even had a little budgie who waltzed when I gave the command. I reckon she was the reincarnation of Pavlova.

The old dog would rest her nose on her paws and the bird would twirl round her while I played The Blue Danube. People came there regularly just to see them and listen to the music.

Having the shop was a bonus because I could sell off all my old gear. In no time at all I'd got rid of the trailer and the tent. Some hippies bought the tent so they could go smoking pot in the bush. A young Chinese bloke took over The Electric Lady, but I doubt he had the know-how to really do well with her. You needed a lot of technical knowledge for The Lady and the right class of woman to go with the outfit too. No one bought The Fishbowl, it was too complicated and too artistic for the present day audience. The Coffin hung around for a while but finally a magician from Wollongong took it over.

I was clapping myself on the back for having got shot of all that lot when a bloke came in with a Lipp piano, asking me to sell it on commission.

That Lipp piano really started the ball rolling. After that the shop filled up with pictures and furniture that people left, hoping I'd make a sale for them one day, and after I had spent a bit of time around the auctions and opportunity shops I soon had enough to keep me going non-stop.

The pressure went off me for the first time in my life. Even if I didn't make a fortune in the shop there were always the evenings at The Cross. I made more than enough to keep myself going.

Of course, not everyone liked having me around up there. There was a publican who got me shifted because he reckoned people gave me too much money ... 'spoilt his trade', he had the nerve to say. And some folks can get very nasty. One bloke in the flats over the way reckoned my playing kept him awake, and he got me in the leg with his air rifle.

The nastiest time I ever had was when a drunk came up one evening when I was sitting playing at the El Alamein Fountain. He tossed an empty beer can at the budgies, and sent them all over the place. I could see he meant business so I stopped playing and quietly collected the little birds up and put them back in their box. He began yelling and laughing, no one in the crowd took a blind bit of notice – I reckon they were scared of interfering with a drunk.

He must have thought he'd got me on the run. I walked over very quick and put a lock round his neck and had him in that fountain before he knew what'd happened. I ducked him up and down and soused him really well before I let him scramble out. How the crowd roared as he ran off! Then I took out the little birds and finished the act.

There are some rotten dingoes in this world, I can tell you. Mind you, there are some lovely people too, like that social worker lady who came round a few days after I'd had my bad turn. No one knew what to do about me.

'You shouldn't be living here all on your own, Mr Lloyd,' she said.

'I've got the dog for company.'

'That's not much help, is it?'

'I'll be right, no need to worry.'

'Now be reasonable ... this could happen again ... you might not be so lucky next time.'

'I'll be right.'

'How can you know that?'

I'd have liked to tell her but I knew she'd never believe me. She'd put me down as going senile or something. But I knew. I knew because when I took that turn I finally met up with the Spirit of the Unknown. I didn't see Him, but as I lay in my bed the room was filled with a great light.

I never actually laid eyes on him, but I knew He was waiting for me, all right.

'Follow me,' He said. 'It's time to leave all this behind you.'

'It's no good. I'm not ready to come. I've got my responsibilities.'

'Who are you to question the ways of Creation?' He asked.

'I've got the birds and the dog, I can't leave them.'

'One day you'll have your animals again but they are not ready and you are.'

'Well that's nice to know,' I told him, 'because there's many who don't believe animals go where we are bound for. But still it's not good enough. If you took me tonight it might be days before anyone called in and who'd feed them? Who'd take the dog out for a walk? No. It's just not on. And while we're about it, who are you, where do you come from? ... I've always known you were around, but I never thought I'd get a chance to talk to you.'

'I was always close to you. I've followed you every day of your life. Who do you think warned you when that Irishman tried to murder you? Who found the little brown bird for you? Who stopped you from going beyond that locked door in Zanzibar? Who has always shown you the way? Trust me and come now.'

'Not without the dog and the birds.'

'They are not ready to leave this earth.'

'Well, I'm not coming then. I won't leave them alone.'

There was a long pause, the light seemed to glow even brighter and then it waned a little.

When He spoke again His voice was very serious. 'People do not argue with me.'

'It's because I'm not ready.'

'You'd prefer that old dog and those dancing birds to the joy of the Unknown?'

'While they need me. I'll come when I'm ready.'

'Well, I can say no more. Stay on your troubled earth, exist in your cold home. Look after your dog and play your fiddle for the little birds but I will come again and when I come next time you'll all go together.'

Epilogue

Owen recovered from his first bout of illness and continued to work at Kings Cross.

Over the next few years he began to find his secondhand business too demanding and gradually disposed of all the stock, spending more time busking at The Cross. Unlike present times, the city council actively discouraged buskers, and Owen's life became increasingly hard as he was frequently told to move on and fined for parking in the wrong place.

He was unfailingly cheerful. He set up his act outside shops and in arcades and even managed to get back to his beloved El Alamein Fountain when the police weren't watching. He was philosophical, as always, but sometimes said 'I've had my day ... they're all young kids ... they don't want me any more.'

Imagine the excitement among all the buskers when the official attitude to street performers underwent a change. Sydney needed a more sophisticated image ... street performers were to be found in all the big cities of the world and we had to take our place in their ranks.

Owen was thrilled to hear that the ABC was planning a 'Best of the Buskers Competition' in 1979. He polished his fiddle, rehearsed the birds and put on his smartest hat. He was sure that such professionals as the ABC staff would recognise a true showman when they saw one.

He came back utterly disheartened ... 'They gave the prize to one of those guitar playing kids ... all long hair and shaking hips. That's the end of it, my day's gone, long gone.'

But his day was not gone. Viewers were so incensed when they saw that such an original, skilful act had been passed over in favour of yet another rock and roller that they wrote in ... and in large numbers too.

The ABC asked Owen back to the studios, re-recorded the session and gave him a special category, all his own, entitled 'Viewers' Choice.'

After that life cheered up for Owen again. No longer was he
harassed by officialdom and he returned to the El Alamein
Fountain.

Owen eventually retired to New Zealand in the early 1980's
and spent his last few years happily living with his children.

Victoria Press is a publishing imprint of The Law Printer. Our aim is to make Victoria, its people, places and activities a more visible part of our lives.

A Field Guide to Victoria's Native Grasslands   **$17.95**
A full-colour reference to the herbs, lilies and wildflowers of our grasslands.
 ISBN 0 7241 8441 4

Koorie   **$12.00**
Tracing the history of Victoria's indigenous people. ISBN 0 7241 9810 5

Settlers Under Sail   **$9.95**
A graphic account of the days of the sailing ship. ISBN 0 7241 8432 5

The Making of Champions   **$12.95**
In-depth interviews with 27 of Australia's top sportswomen. ISBN 0 7241 8444 9

Forgotten Heroes: Aborigines at War from the Somme to Vietnam   **$19.95**
Telling the stories of black servicemen and women. ISBN 0 7241 8456

Beekeeping   **$15.00**
For beginners and professional apiarists. ISBN 0 7241 9839 3

What On Earth Can We Do?   **$14.95**
A Handbook of Careers that Care for the Environment
The career book for the nineties. ISBN 0 7241 8435 X

Crosbie Morrison: Voice of Nature   **$26.95**
The story of a well-known and loved Victorian naturalist. ISBN 0 7241 8443 0

Cops, Crooks and Catastrophes   **$12.95**
Hilarious tales from the mouths of Victorian police officers.
ISBN 0 7241 8446 5

A Gallery of Plants   **$9.95**
A comprehensive guide to the plant collections in the Royal Botanic Gardens.
ISBN 0 7241 8446 5

Treasures of Victoria Postcards   **$6.50**
Displaying a range of Victoria's treasures.

Phar Lap: A Brief History   **$5.95**
The career of Australia's best galloper, the 'Anzac Antelope'.
ISBN 0 7241 8434 1

Port of Many Prows
Traces the fascinating history of the port of Williamstown. $25.00
ISBN 0 7241 8464 1

Steam Power in Victoria $24.95
A history of the social improvements brought about by the steam age.
ISBN 0 7241 8465 1

A Special Madness $16.95
A Celebration of the thirtieth anniversary of The Beatles' Australian tour.
ISBN 0 7241 8459 7

An Australian Pilgrimage $19.95
The story of Muslims in Australia, from the seventeenth century to the present.
ISBN 0 7241 8450 3

Common Insects and Spiders of Victoria $15.95
A full-colour guide to the bugs of Victoria's backyards and bush.
ISBN 0 7241 8466 X

**Victoria Press titles are distributed by The Law Printer,
PO Box 292, South Melbourne 3205. Telephone: (03) 242 4600**